Contents

Part One - Getting Ready

Part Two - Activities

First Year Categories

Second Year Categories

Third Year Categories

Acknowledgements

In the past two decades hundreds of middle level schools have instituted teacher advisory programs. Faculties or faculty committees in those schools have developed materials for use in such programs. Consultants have frequently shared their ideas and expertise in workshops. To meet the almost desperate need of faculties ideas and activities were "begged, borrowed, or stolen." They were often taken verbatim from existing sources or altered by the teachers to suit their situations.

It is not now possible to acknowledge the original source of these various activities. They have been adapted and used by many faculties. Listed below are the schools and individuals that to the best of our knowledge participated at some point in developing the materials from which the contents of Part Two of this source book were derived. There are undoubtedly other individuals and sources that should be recognized for their contributions. No oversight is intentional.

Blankenship, William. *Advisement Handbook,* Westminster High School, Westminster, CA

Colten, Anne. *Student Advisement.* University High School, Irvine, CA

Cowles, Robert J. *Advisement.* Ferguson Reorganized School District R-11, Florissant, MO

George, Paul, University of Florida, Gainesville

George Reed Middle School, New Castle, DE

Glasser, William. *Schools Without Failure.* Harper & Row, New York.

Holdorf, Linda. Gregory Middle School, Naperville, IL

Lipham, James M. & Daresh, John C. *Teacher Advisor Programs.* Wisconsin Research & Development Center for Individualized Schooling, 1980.

Matakovich, Mary. *Advisement.* Ocean View High School, Huntington Beach, CA

Mirenzi, Joseph. *TAP.* Anne Arundel County Public Schools, Annapolis, MD

Raritan High School, Hazlet Township Public School District, Hazlet, NJ

Red Clay Consolidated School District, Wilmington, DE

Shue Middle School, Christina School District, Newark, DE 19711

SMASH: A Middle School Guidance Curriculum, Patapsco Middle School, Howard County Public Schools, Columbia, MD 1979.

Teacher Advisor Program Handbook. Montgomery County Public Schools, Rockville, MD

Vancouver Public School, School District #37, Vancouver, WA

White Bear Mariner High School, White Bear Lake, MN

Wilde Lake High School, Howard County, Columbia, MD

Part I

Getting Ready

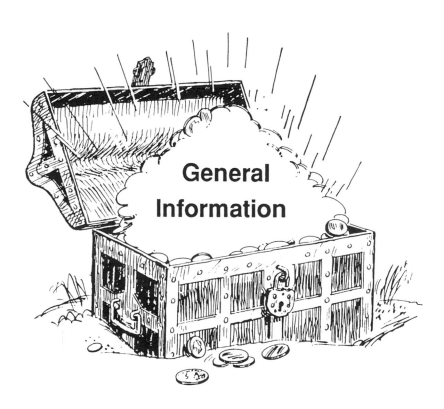

General

Information

How to Use This Source Book

This is a source book, not a curriculum. An exemplary teacher advisory program grows more out of the student-teacher relationship than out of the materials used. The activities and content are means to ends and not ends themselves.

While the materials and the 120 activities provided herein are most likely to be used in a teacher advisory program they certainly are not limited to use there. The several getting acquainted activities, for instance, are appropriate for use by any teacher as new classes are getting underway. Many of the other activities are especially valuable for use in academic classes at particular times. For instance, the fishbowl activity (p. 156) is one of several that would be useful when a class is going to move into cooperative group activities.

It would behoove all middle level teachers to become thoroughly familiar with the contents of this source book, reviewing the general materials in Part One and then gaining a familiarity with the many activities provided in Part Two, many of which are appropriate in regular class and team settings.

Activities: The heart of the source book

Part Two of this source book is comprised of three sections or divisions. Each of the three sections includes 40 activities organized by categories. Advisers can select the one or ones most appropriate for their group from each category. Advisers should, of course, also modify and adjust the activities to meet their situation.

The detailed list of specific activities divided into categories is shown at the beginning of each section. These activities were selected from a large pool of several hundred. Multi-graded advisories would use Section One the first year, Section Two the next, and Section Three the third year. This format would enable sixth graders to participate in activities through the eighth grade without repeating any specific activity.

Advisory groups that consist of a single grade would use Section One in the sixth grade, Section Two in the seventh grade, and Section Three in the eighth grade. The first year a program is initiated, regardless of the grade level, advisers would probably want to start with Section One, although some activities from other divisions might be selected.

Activities generally take 1-2 sessions to complete, based on a 25 minute advisory period. The adviser's discretion should determine the amount of time spent on any given topic.

Because interpersonal skills directly affect a person's quality of life, the majority of the activities utilize group dynamics. It is our hope that students will become more successful in their relationships by learning to appreciate and respect the differences among cultures and people.

With the help of a caring advisor and activities selected from this book, middle school students should be better prepared to cope with the complexities of today's world. Through increased self-awareness and improved self-esteem, the middle years can be a more positive and less stressful experience for the youth negotiating them.

Why Have A TA Program?

All middle level teachers are advisors. It cannot be otherwise, for the developmental needs of young adolescents are pressing and omnipresent. It is impossible to establish the comfortable student-teacher relationship that is needed for successfully conducting the academic business of the middle school without also being concerned with the social, emotional, and physical development of the students.

While we separate out for discussion purposes these several areas of development, they are inexorably intertwined in the lives of young adolescents. Classroom concern for affective factors cannot be put aside in order to concentrate on academic achievement concerns. As James (NMSA, 1986) has stated: "... no learning situation or teaching process is without its inseparable affective attributes." To learn best, young adolescents need to be connected; to feel a sense of personal relationship with the teacher, and to feel known and recognized as individuals. It should be said as well that no false dichotomy should be created when a teacher advisory program is instituted. Such programs are extremely important and needed but they should not be used as an excuse for failure to recognize the importance of the affective aspects of the regular classes. Establishing connections with students is challenging and teachers are continually in search of ideas and resources that help. This volume is dedicated to that end.

Our knowledge of this critical period in the human life cycle also makes it clear that young adolescents are deeply concerned about and very much occupied with their physical, psychological, and social development. Like it or not, it is simply a reality that school programs designed for 10-14 year olds must address and accommodate. This is not to say that their intellectual development and academic progress take a back seat, but rather that in order to insure maximum academic achievement schools must also help youth meet their psychosocial developmental needs.

Youth in the period of early adolescence are vulnerable. They are leaving the security of childhood, but are still years and many new experiences away from the maturity of full adolescence. They need the security, support, and understanding of adults as they work their way through the several developmental tasks faced during this stage. Surveys of youth consistently point out the depth and extent of their concern with grades, personal relationships, physical development, and current major societal issues such as nuclear war and alcoholism.

"The most important ideas any man ever has are the ideas about himself.
— Robert Bills

"Cognitive learning cannot take place in a state of affective disorder, and we can no longer assume that the family or some other agency will take responsibility for the student's (total) affective development. It is imperative that school systems devote both their wits and their financial resources to the production of programs of affective learning.
— A. Mikalachi in *Orbit* 1973

The typical intermediate school curriculum, largely pre-determined and packaged, rarely touches on these personal and social concerns of youth. A major characteristic of newer middle schools, therefore, has been some form of a teacher advisory program. Variously called advisor-advisee, homebase, or by locally established labels such as Prime Time, these programs all seek to provide a time and a place for a group of students and a professional leader to interact. The leader has special responsibility as an advocate for these students to help them deal with concerns not normally acknowledged in other class settings, primarily those associated with the affective domain.

Middle level educators have consistently recommended an organizational structure which ensures that every individual student in a middle level school has one adult who knows that individual well and can be an understanding advocate. Parents, likewise, have wanted the assurance that there is an adult available who truly knows their child and can provide the personal attention their young adolescent needs. In fact, Garvin (*Middle School Journal,* November 1987) when interviewing parents, found that in response to the question "What would you like for the middle level school to provide for your child?" the second most frequently cited type of response was "I want to know that when my child is in school that he/she knows at least one adult well enough to go to if support is needed."

Early junior high schools were not unmindful of such needs and, in fact, pioneered in the development of homeroom programs. These homerooms originally designed to be teacher advisory programs with broad responsibilities, became, over time, administrative homerooms concerned almost exclusively with attendance, textbook distribution, lunch tickets, and announcements.

The middle school movement has championed the renaissance of the original homeroom, and next to interdisciplinary teaming, teacher advisory programs have become the most frequently cited characteristic of a true middle school. While such programs differ very widely in their character, curriculum, and organization they are united in their commitment to providing additional affirmation, assistance, and support to young adolescent learners.

Self-definition is facilitated by being with people who know us well and who give us useful information about ourselves.
— David Elkind, 1984

*He drew a circle
that shut me out
Heretic, rebel, a thing
to flout
But love and I had
the wit to win
We drew a circle that
took him in.*
— Edwin Markham

"If you treat an individual as he is, he will stay as he is, but if you treat him as if he were what he ought to be and could be, he will become what he ought to be and what he could be."
— Goethe

Widespread Advocacy for TA Programs

The middle school child needs one adult at school to whom he can go for information and assistance regarding any problem... a plan whereby each child is a member of a homebase group led by a teacher-counselor seems desirable.

Alexander and others,
The Emergent Middle School, 1969, p. 66

Every student should have access to at least one adult who knows and cares for him personally, and who is responsible for helping him to deal with problems of growing up.

Lounsbury and Vars, A Curriculum for
the Middle School Years, 1978, p. 41

Each transescent learner needs an adult who knows him or her well and is in a position to give individual attention... Homebase or advisor-advisee programs which provide ...regular opportunities for interaction with a small group of peers and a caring adult fill this need.

This We Believe, NMSA, 1982, p. 12-13

To achieve needed student development, schools must institute advisement programs that assure each student regular, compassionate, and supportive counsel from a concerned adult about his or her academic process, adjustment to school and personal adjustment.

An Agenda for Excellence at the
Middle Level, NASSP, 1985, p. 4

Every student should be well known by at least one adult. Small group advisories, homerooms, or other arrangements enable teachers or other staff members to provide guidance and actively monitor the academic and social development of students.

Turning Points,
Carnegie Corporation, 1989, p. 40

"In no other stage of the life cycle, are the promises of finding oneself and the threat of losing oneself so closely allied."
— Erik Erikson, 1963

"Treat a child as though he already is the person he is capable of becoming.
— Haim Ginott

"Flatter me, and I may not believe you. Criticize me, and I may not like you. Ignore me, and I may not forgive you. Encourage me, and I will not forget you.
— Wm. Arthur Ward

What Are the Objectives of the Program?

All of the objectives of middle level education are served in some way by a teacher advisory program. Though the emphasis may be on those objectives most related to the affective domain which are typically not served well in the regular curriculum, it is wrong to assume that such programs exist *only* to assist students in their psychosocial development. Direct and indirect assistance in the mastery of academic information, the refinement of old skills and the learning of new ones, the exploration of interest areas, and the ascertaining of student aptitudes are all components of a teacher advisory program.

Many people assume falsely that advisory programs require teachers to be counselors. They do not. Advising and counseling, although closely related, are not the same. Claire Cole, a former middle school counselor, clarified the distinction between the two in these statements.

> Counseling involves behavior change of a very specific nature where something is identified as a concern and the counselor and the student lay out a program together that helps the behavior change occur. There is evaluation and follow-up in specialized kinds of techniques. Advising is a much lower level of involvement with students in the sense that you're not necessarily working on behavior change. Advisory would much more likely be working on things that are more common to all students.

from *Middle Link*, CEYA, Spring 1991, p. 1

A teacher advisory program does not reduce the need for professional counselors nor does it replace them. On the other hand, the nature of young adolescents calls for more "advising" and personal support than a counselor with the typical load of 350 students can possibly give.

The specific objectives of teacher advisory programs vary, and in fact are preferably generated at the school level. Those identified in the previous section, and those listed below reflect frequently articulated broad objectives that can serve as guiding examples.

"The irreducible essence of teacher advisory is a commitment to kids."
— Chris Stevenson, 1991

"The advisory program complements the school guidance program by providing students with daily interaction with an adult mentor, but does not replace the need for guidance counselors."
— Texas Task Force on Middle School Education, 1991

"There is no one up there to talk to."
— (Comment of a former middle school advisee on the high school)

Objectives of Advisory

1. Provide an environment and activities that will foster bonding within an advisory group so that students will feel accepted and valued by teacher and peers.

2. Help students cope with academic concerns and set goals which will facilitate positive school experiences.

3. Give students avenues through which to discover their uniqueness so that they might come to appreciate the many differences among people.

4. Help students develop positive relationships through experiences that utilize group dynamics.

5. Promote critical thinking skills through discussion and problem solving activities so that students can learn to make responsible choices.

6. Develop listening skills and an understanding of the road blocks which hinder effective communication.

7. Build self-esteem in students so that they might become confident, capable young people who accept responsibility for their own actions.

8. Heighten student awareness of good citizenship through providing opportunities for meaningful contributions to their school and community.

9. Provide opportunities for extensive student involvement through shared decision making.

10. Improve home/school communication and relationships.

"We won't get the best from our junior high students until we stop blaming adolescents for their adolescent behavior."
— Nancy Atwell

"The greatest discovery of my generation is that human beings can alter their lives by altering their attitudes of mind."
— William James

"Just as students have relatively untapped resources for learning and development, so educators have relatively untapped resources for encouraging this development."
— William W. Purkey & John Novak, *Inviting School Success*, 1984

Getting Off to a Good Start

"You never get a second chance to make a first impression."

First impressions are paramount, so the tone set in the first meeting or two of an advisory group or a regular class is vital. And the advisor is the one who is both able to and responsible for setting the climate of the class. In an advisory group it is especially important that students feel completely comfortable in the setting.

In order to get youngsters to open up and to share their concerns and questions, it is best for the advisor to lead the way. While teachers have traditionally thought it proper to remain somewhat aloof from students, service as an advisor calls for a more personal relationship. The initial self-disclosure by the teacher of some aspects of his or her being sets the stage for this to occur. Doing such obvious things as telling the advisees about one's family, home, prior cities of residence, and colleges attended is a beginning point. Excellent also is the sharing of pictures of the advisor during his/her early adolescent years, artifacts from high school days, or things created by a hobby. Bringing a family member (mother, sibling, spouse, etc.) to the class as a guest provides much excitement and elicits many questions about what the advisor was like as an adolescent or is now as an adult.

If students are to interview one another as an initial get-acquainted activity the advisor might well be the first person interviewed. The task of developing a list of questions for those interviews is a good means of achieving early on the kind of interaction and free exchange sought. Needed are questions personal enough to yield interesting information but not inappropriately personal, ones that would yield some comparative data that could be organized and tabulated to provide a group profile and some common ground.

The more the advisor can become a regular member of the group sharing in appropriate activities the better. The advisor must not, of course, overdo involvement and dominate, but establishing an atmosphere of relative intimacy is essential.

The importance of getting off to a good start warrants special thought and attention, not just in the activity selected but in the climate established.

Suggestions for Making Discussions Click

Students like to talk, but they often lack the skills needed to participate in a free-flowing rap session. These should help.

1. Precede all discussions with some "doing;" an art activity, story, film, exercise.

2. Conduct most discussion groups in pairs, trios or quads so that students talk about the topic in small, groups.

3. Assign group roles and responsibilities for students (e.g.: recorder, reporter, encourager, clarifier).

4. Use 3"X5" cards to help format your discussions via these steps:

• Each student is given 3 cards and asked to put one respose to the statement/question on each of the cards. (Example — the theme could be, "I worry about...")

• Then form groups of 5-7

• The groups read all the shuffled cards aloud in a circular fashion, laying the cards out in order to identify common feelings and ideas, then record on paper a "We worry about.." list, and presents their list to the class.

• It's possible to stop here and draw general conclusions about the common concerns or you can plan further discussion around one common theme with hopes of discovering resolutions and solutions.

5. Practice specific discussion skills in small groups. Have students work on a skill such as paraphrasing and then have them also evaluate their success. These mini-lessons will prove useful when you venture into regular discussion groups.

How Should a TA Program Be Organized?

There is no "standard" or "right" way to organize a TA program. There are many options, each with advantages and disadvantages. Faculty readiness, time pressures, central office support, community acceptance, faculty leadership — all are factors that affect decisions about how a TA program should be organized.

How often and when should the group meet?

A utopian answer would be ten times a week, twice a day, first thing in the morning for about 25 minutes and the last thing in the day for about 7 minutes. There are some schools that do provide such a schedule. A much less-than-satisfactory minimum would be once a week for 25 minutes. There must be, however, a definite, regularly scheduled time within the school day when the adviser and the advisees can be together. When it is the first thing in the day, the program assumes the routine responsibilities of homerooms — attendance, announcements, etc. The Student Council may be composed of a representative from each advisory.

Some schools schedule their TA programs in the middle of the morning, some coordinate it with the lunch period so the adviser and advisees can eat together. Some schedule it at the end of the day, which when judiciously orchestrated, can be a wonderful way to reflect on a full day's events. Schools often extend the regular homeroom 15 or 20 minutes once or twice a week to create an advisory period.

Many schools schedule an advisory period two or three times a week. Those that provide an everyday schedule usually restrict so-called affective activities to twice a week using the other days for silent reading, individual conferences, and other special activities such as intramurals. Important, however, is the continuity of caring that exists when the adviser and the advisees are in regular communication, become comfortable with one another, and share a variety of experiences together.

How large should the group be?

To facilitate an atmosphere of intimacy a group of 12-15 students is widely recommended. In order to achieve such a relatively small number, schools must use virtually all certified personnel as advisers. In other cases, only the academic core teachers serve as advisers which means their groups run as high as 25, or even 30. Teachers in such cases feel that the large number is a handicap somewhat buffeted by the fact that they advise the students they

> "Self-esteem is not something we give kids. It's what we have to stop taking away."
> — Hancock McCarty
> in *Teacher*, May/June '91

> "Although advisees give me some sleepless nights worrying about them and their problems and their choices, it feels good to have a group you can call your own for the three years they travel through my life and change from children to adolescents."
> — Sally Willett, Teacher-adviser, University of Northern Colorado Lab School, Greeley, CO

teach. Many successful programs have groups in the 18-25 range, but these high numbers do limit the nature of workable activities, and indeed can restrict the level of intimacy that can be achieved. Ultimately, the decision as to the size of the advisory group has to be made in light of local factors. Generally speaking, however, smallness is to be desired.

How are students grouped?

Groups may be composed of students from one grade level or they may be multi-graded with some sixth, seventh, and eighth graders all present. They may be arbitrarily placed in groups by the administration; or the students themselves may have a major role in choosing the groups they are assigned to; or groups may be constituted by their first period class assignment; or the team of teachers may divide their students into groups.

Multi-graded groups in which one-third of the students (8th graders) leave each year and are replaced by sixth graders provide nicely for a continuity of caring and much peer support. So too do arrangements in which advisors, regardless of the grade level of their teaching assignment, start with an advisory group of sixth graders who then remain with them for three years. An advisor who has the same advisees for three years certainly comes to know them well. On the other hand, others believe that the personal-social needs of kids are better served when the TA group is composed of just one grade level and the advisees have, presumably, much the same concerns and interests. Moreover, while a three year relationship is remarkably enriching, many teachers feel they are more effective advisors when they advise students they teach. This allows teachers to assist students with homework, coach their academic progress, and deal directly with their daily concerns. It is important that advisors maintain contact with school specialists and any teachers not serving as advisors.

Who's in charge?

Most frequently, a counselor assumes overall responsibility for the TA program. With backgrounds and professional preparation in guidance, counselors are logical choices for leadership. A small faculty committee frequently works with the counselor in monitoring and supporting the program. Sometimes an administrator assumes responsibility for guiding the program.

"Well, I must endure the presence of two or three caterpillars if I wish to become acquainted with the butterflies. "
— *The Little Prince*
Antoine de Saint Exupery

U.S. Teens' Top Ten Issues

Based on 9,000 letters from seventh and eighth grade students to their U.S. representatives.

Drug Abuse	**17%**
The Homeless	**5%**
Environment	**15%**
Child Abuse	**4%**
Sexual Issues	**13%**
Suicide	**3%**
Violence	**8%**
Alcohol Abuse	**3%**
Education	**6%**
AIDS	**3%**

What Comprises a TA Curriculum?

Activities and experiences that are appropriate fare for teacher advisory programs comprise a vast array. The possibilities are, indeed, almost unlimited. They range from activities that are very academic in nature to others that are admittedly purely recreational. They may focus on skills or on personal behaviors.

Pre-planned and organized activities provide most of the substance of the curriculum. Such activities tend to deal more with the affective than the cognitive domain, as do the activities that comprise the three divisions of this source book.

In addition, there are a host of other activities and experiences which can be the basis for valuable TA sessions. No extensive preparation of materials or the possession of particular skills are needed to conduct most TA activities.

The list below outlines some of the many possibilities that exist. In reading these open-ended advisory ideas, other activities may well come to mind.

1.   Arrange to meet with the principal, preferably in the administrative area, for an informal Q&A session about what is involved in running a school.

2.   Comparable sessions can be scheduled with the cafeteria manager, the custodian, or other service persons.

3.   Have students give two minute extemporaneous talks on topics drawn out of a hat — a fun activity that provides needed practice in oral communication.

4.   Have students write a friendly letter to a relative, out-of-town friend, or other person that wouldn't normally be contacted regularly.

5.   Initiate correspondence with an advisory group in another state.

6.   Plan and carry out an in-school breakfast for the advisory group.

7.   Invite two or three parents (not of students in the group) to come in for a discussion of parent-child relations.

8.   The daily newspaper provides a basis for discussing the geography of the news, how to interpret the editorial page cartoon, what job

Types of Typical TA Activities

Orientation to the school

Getting acquainted

Self-esteem and self-evaluation

Social and group dynamics skills

Study skills and academic assistance

Journal and/or creative writing

Silent or oral reading

Service and community

Career planning

Discussions on issues and concerns of kids

opportunities exist in our community, or one of a number of such possibilities. Many papers carry 'Today in History" which makes good grist for a review of history and/or a discussion on "which event has had the greatest effect on history?" (For instance, on March 5 these events occurred: in 1946, Winston Churchhill gave his "Iron Curtain" address; in 1982, Comedian John Belushi died of a drug overdose; in 1984, the Supreme Court ruled that public funds could be used for a nativity scene as a part of a display without violating the separation of church and state; and in 1990, workers in Bucharest, Romania succeeded in removing a 25-foot, 7-ton statue of Lenin from its foundation.)

9.   Listen to commercially made tapes of good literature. Sherlock Holmes is a possibility.

10.   Decide on and carry out a school service project such as posters for the cafeteria, landscaping part of the campus, or an anti-litter campaign.

11.   Have volunteer students discuss their hobbies, showing samples and demonstrating as appropriate.

12.   Invite interesting resource persons to share a session. Possibilities include a recently discharged service person, an EMT, a senior citizen, a downtown merchant, or a government official.

"Take the PP out of AA."

This cleverly phrased principle enunciated by Sandra Schurr makes a major point — take the paper and pencil out of advisor-advisee.

Because teacher advisory programs are new and teachers have not normally received any training for directing such programs they have been difficult to implement and sustain. Teachers need and should have ample resources on which to draw; however, a real teacher advisory program uses such activities judiciously not completely. Too often teachers become overly reliant on canned activities and handouts and a new version of the old "purple curriculum" results. Hence, Sandra Schurr's recommendation.

The ultimate curriculum for a teacher advisory program is that one which a particular group of advisees under the direction of their advisor design. When an advisory group reaches that stage of rapport,

Resources for Read Aloud

People   Peter Spier

The Book of Questions and *The Kids' Book of Questions*
            Gregory Stock

Winners and Losers
            Sydney Harris

The Velveteen Rabbit
            Margery Williams

Gorilla   Anthony Browne

The Giving Tree
            Shel Silverstein

The Hating Book
            Charlotte Zolotow

Arthur's Teacher Trouble
            Marc Brown

Leo The Late Bloomer
            Robert Kraus

The Dinosaur's Divorce
            Laurene Kransny Brown
            & Marc Brown

Alexander and the Terrible, Horrible, No Good, Very Bad Day   Judith Viorst

Miss Nelson Is Back
            James Marshall

The Fall of Freddie the Leaf
            Leo Buscaglia

The Precious Present
            Spencer Johnson

Funny Insults and Snappy Put Downs   Joseph Rosenbloom

Don't Worry, Be Happy
            Bobby McFerrin

A Family Is A Circle of People Who Love You
            Doris Jasinek

What To Do When You're Feeling Blue
Mark Schneider & Ellen Meyer

Harold And The Purple Crayon
            Crockett Johnson

The Hug Therapy Book and *Hug Therapy 2*
            Kathleen Keating

The Little Prince
            Antoine de Saint Exupery

intimacy, and initiative that makes it possible for them to establish their own curriculum something close to utopia has been achieved.

Such a stage of group cohesiveness and maturity does not occur easily or quickly — but it is a goal that every advisory should keep before it. Particularly when a group of advisees maintain the same advisor over the three years of the middle school it is an achievable goal.

The need to provide adequate structure, teacher security, and resources usually leads to the establishment of themes for each month. For instance, the Amery (Wisconsin) Middle School uses these school-wide monthly themes:

August	Getting Acquainted
September	Study Skills
October	Self-esteem
November	Friendships and Family Conferences
December	Community Involvement
January	Career/Goal Setting
February	Interpersonal Communications
March	Problem Solving and Conflict Resolutions
April	Self-awareness/Positive Attitudes
May	End of Year Wrap-up

You spoke to me of love, I doubted you.

You spoke to me of caring, I doubted you.

You spoke to me of my self-worth; I doubted you.

You came to the hospital to visit me, I believed everything you said.

— Robert Ricken, *Love Me When I'm Most Unlovable,* NASSP, 1984.

The Gregory Middle School in Naperville, Illinois has established these themes for its Teacher Advisory Program (TAP):

6th Grade	7th Grade	8th Grade
School orientation and adjustment	TAP, Team and School Identity	TAP, Team and School Identity
TAP, Team and School Identity	Goal Setting and Self-management	Academic Survival Skills
Self-concept	Value Awareness	Self-concept
Relationships	Value Awareness	Leadership
Appreciating Differences	Conflict Resolution	Decision Making
Accepting Responsibility	Failure and Competition	Look to the Future
Decision Making	Growing Pains and Pleasures	
School, Community, Global Awareness	Community Service	
Saying Goodbye	Decision Making	
Study Skills Reinforcement		

Regardless of whether themes are established or not, much improvisation and creativity on the part of the advisor are essential. Always to be kept in mind too is the importance of actively involving the students in planning and carrying out the TA program.

How To Keep An Advisory Notebook

A Successful Adviser Explains

Sally Willett

University of Northern Colorado Lab School, Greeley, Colorado

Being an advisor to a group of middle schoolers requires a lot of juggling. As scattered files and correspondence with students, other teachers, and parents accumulates, it is vital to find a method for organizing materials so they are accessible and easy to maintain. A well-organized advisory notebook will become an indispensable tool for keeping group and individual student information together. In designing the notebook, think about the roles that are required of an advisor and what information would need to be included.

I have found that two basic parts—*advisor* record-keeping and *advisee* information — are needed.

PART I

I divided this part into five sections. The first section is labeled "Student Info" and has an alphabetical list of all advisees, their parents names and phone numbers, and minicourses or exploratory class enrolled in. (As these classes change, staple a clean paper over this column to include new classes.) This reference sheet will be helpful when making parent calls and when trying to quickly track down students during exploratory periods.

The second section includes attendance records. As an advisor it's important to know which students are absent, when, and for what reasons so that contact with parents and other teachers can be made if absences affect learning.

The third section contains calendars for keeping track of plans and special activities. An overall monthly calendar includes school-wide activities such as flex days, assemblies, book talks, major academic projects, sports or drama events, and special advisor responsibilities such as lunch or bus duties. Another weekly planning calendar focuses on activities specifically for advisory periods. For this calendar I use a format that has a Monday-Friday schedule with one or two weeks on a side. Besides using it as a planner for the week, it can be used to make notes about the success of an activity or to list students who have conference appointments. Included on this page is a place for reminders or ideas for other activities.

The fourth section contains copies of advisee worksheets or activities that will be used during the upcoming weeks. Also included in this section is a "think sheet" where ideas for future discussion, activities, or projects can be jotted down for later use or development. An "overdue homework" assignment sheet might be included in this section so a quick check can be made with the group as to what assignments are late and appropriate follow-up can be pursued.

The fifth section is a miscellaneous one in which I file copies of schedules, announcements, school policies, and special forms as well as class lists.

PART II

The second part of the notebook is for keeping information on individual advisees. Each advisee has a divider section. Keep records simple, following the same format for all students. Combine information on one page when possible and use both sides of a page for the same topic.

The first sheet in each student's section is a more complete Student Information page. It includes name, birthday, age, home address, home phone, parents' names, work phones, places of employment, and emergency numbers. A half page is usually sufficient.

```
┌─────────────────────────────────────────┐
│          STUDENT INFORMATION             │
│                                          │
│   NAME:                                  │
│                                          │
│   BIRTHDAY              AGE               │
│                                          │
│   HOME ADDRESS                           │
│                                          │
│                                          │
│   HOME PHONE #                           │
│                                          │
│   PARENTS: NAME        WORK PHONE #      │
│   PLACE OF WORK:                         │
│   NAME:                WORK PHONE #      │
│   PLACE OF WORK:                         │
│                                          │
└─────────────────────────────────────────┘
```

The second sheet is entitled **Organization Skills** and includes these topics: *Notebook Check* and *Locker Clean-up* on the top half of the paper (note date when periodic checks are made of notebooks and lockers to insure they are regularly cleaned out, reorganized, and resupplied if necessary), and *Homework and Overdue Assignments* on the bottom half. Transfer students' missing assignments from the advisor section to this list so that when conferencing with students or parents there is a complete record of overdue assignments. It's helpful to keep notes stating why assignments were late or if there were special circumstances for being overdue. Periodically send out a list of your advisees to other teachers and request notification if assignments are overdue or if there are other concerns or compliments to share. Help other advisors by reciprocating.

```
┌─────────────────────────────────────────┐
│          ORGANIZATIONAL SKILLS           │
│                                          │
│   NAME:                                  │
│                                          │
│   NOTEBOOK CHECK    LOCKER CLEANUP       │
│                                          │
│                                          │
│   HOMEWORK AND OVERDUE ASSIGNMENTS       │
│                                          │
└─────────────────────────────────────────┘
```

The next sheet, **Personal Learning Plans,** records students' goals. The top of the page has three columns: *Date, Goal,* and *Date Completed.* (This sheet would not be the implementation worksheet a student would complete as the goal was formulated, but a quick review for the adviser's use.) Most advisory programs include goal-setting for students as an important skill to develop. Also many schools are involving students in planning personal learning programs which are based on academic and personal goals. This sheet would serve as a tool to keep track of goals set and to monitor the continuing development of this skill. It is a positive way to maintain an open dialogue with students and to discuss and encourage goal-setting and completion. As parents become active in this process, this record will help during conferences to quickly summarize the student's progress.

```
┌─────────────────────────────────────────┐
│         PERSONAL LEARNING PLAN           │
│                                          │
│   NAME:                                  │
│                                          │
│   DATE        GOAL        COMPLETED      │
│                                          │
└─────────────────────────────────────────┘
```

The **Student Interaction** page has two columns: *Date* and *Topic & Discussion.* Change in their academic, social, and emotional growth is characteristic of middle level students. Making notes of the trials and triumphs of advisees can assist in the everyday guidance that advisors provide. A log encourages follow-up of problems to see if they have been resolved or need further attention. Notes can also be made that emphasize the positive interactions a student has with others or any change in behavior that is unusual. This log is also a place to note student conferences as well as noting strategies of working with a student or special interests that could be capitalized on at another time and shared with other faculty. Taking time to quickly jot down student interactions will assist in keeping in touch with a student's personal growth.

```
+--------------------------------------------------+
|            STUDENT INTERACTION LOG               |
| NAME                                             |
|                                                  |
| DATE          TOPIC AND DISCUSSION               |
|                                                  |
|                                                  |
|                                                  |
+--------------------------------------------------+
```

sustained reading program, book projects, or reading conferences are part of advisory time, maintain a diary of these activities. Also in each student's section progress reports or contracts can be filed. Information that is strictly confidential should not be kept in this notebook.

Another important page is **Parent Correspondence.** Once again the two columns at the top are *Date and Topic Discussion.* Make note of all parent discussions or conferences and their dates. Often parent phone calls or "hallway" conversations deal with issues that may need to be remembered for future conferences. Keeping track of issues will be valuable in sustaining a dialogue with parents about their student's progress and problems.

```
+--------------------------------------------------+
|               READING CONFERENCES                |
| NAME:                                            |
|                                                  |
| DATE          BOOK          DISCUSSION           |
|                                                  |
+--------------------------------------------------+
```

SOME ADDED TIPS

Use a notebook that has pockets in which to store announcements to be made, collected forms that need to be handed in, and other odds and ends. Try to find dividers that can be written on with pencil and that have small tabs so that seven or eight tabs can be seen easily at a time and a section can be found quickly. If students remain with the same advisor for several years, their section becomes a good chronology of their growth process. If students change advisors yearly, the information could follow the students to their next advisor.

```
+--------------------------------------------------+
|            PARENT CORRESPONDENCE LOG             |
| NAME:                                            |
|                                                  |
| DATE          TOPIC AND DISCUSSION               |
|                                                  |
|                                                  |
|                                                  |
|                                                  |
|                                                  |
+--------------------------------------------------+
```

Other pages in the advisee section would be specific to a school's program. Special projects that a student participated in could be logged. If a silent

The adviser notebook when used consistently can become a valuable resource record. With ample information available on each advisee, the adviser will be better prepared to offer positive feedback and assistance when needed.

There were times when I would stumble and fall. There were the times when a person treasured in my heart forever would be present — my adviser. In his own special and unique way, he would encourage me to never lose sight of my goal and to press on to the top. He taught me to believe in myself; to believe that I have the destiny, the innate ability, to become all I expect in life.

He guided me to search for the meaning of life. He reinforced my personal belief to challenge myself, to always remember that each road I choose will offer some difficulty.

My adviser became more than an inspiration; he became a friend. If it weren't for people such as my adviser, I might never have picked myself up after one of my falls, and I might have lost sight of my vision. The adviser always becomes the family, the parent, of the students while in school.

— Costas Pangopoulos, from his address to the National Association of Student Councils' Conference upon receiving the 1990 Shell Century II Leaders National Award.

Musing About ... Advisory

Ross M. Burkhardt

Shoreham-Wading River Middle School, NY

excerpted from *Transescence* Vol XIX No. 1, 1991

Since 1972, advisory has been a part of my job, and it is impossible to imagine working in a middle school without it. I teach English and social studies to a team of forty-two students, nine of whom are in my advisory.

———————

Advisory permeates the building. Staff members are always looking out for their advisees, meeting with them, counseling, coaching, listening to them, just being there — an adult presence ready to assist if needed. Because of advisory, when teachers meet to talk about kids, the talk goes somewhere: the advisor has that responsibility. Advisory handles much of the discipline in a preventive manner — when every student is being looked after, problems are dealt with before they get out of hand.

———————

After conferences, advisees can no longer be ciphers sitting in the third row, second seat, who have or have not done their homework. Rather, advisees become living, breathing human beings who have many of the same cares and concerns I do. Advisory conferences suggest that all students, not just my advisees, have such concerns; in that sense, my advisees are constant reminders of the humanity of the rest of my students.

———————

Advisory is a constant reminder that our central purpose as middle school teachers is to work directly with kids. While the nature of what we teach and when and how we teach it might change, the direct, one-to-one relationship with individual kids does not. Advisory allows us to be coaches and advocates for kids.

———————

Kids judge advisory differently than adults. They do not appreciate the importance of the conferences so much as they enjoy the little touches — celebrating birthdays, going out for a bagel, doing an activity together such as bowling or a movie. Yet when asked, they provide eloquent testimony to the value of advisory in their lives. Brie commented, "I always looked forward to advisory because it was a place where you could get away in the morning or in the middle of the day when you needed a break from everyone or from your work. I saw it as a place to just relax and hang out. In advisory there was no wrong; you could hang out and be yourself."

———————

Part II

Activities

First Year

Contents I

NOTE: numbers in parentheses indicate number of related handouts

A

Proudly Presenting...

Objective:

To acquaint advisory students with one another, to build rapport

Time:

One session

Procedures:

1. Advisees pair up, preferably with someone they don't know.

2. Partners have five minutes to tell each other things about their hobbies,
    accomplishments, favorite foods, places, family, travels, etc.

3. Reassemble in a circle, but with partners not sitting next to each other.
    In turn, players stand and introduce their partners in as interesting a way as
    possible.

    For example:

    *"I'm very happy to say we have an 'expert' guitar player with us today. He likes to
    fish, swim, and eat chocolate ice cream. May I present ..."*

    (Person introduced stands up and bows as group applauds)

4. After all students have been introduced, see if one or two members can identify everyone
    by first name and with one "fact" about each.

A

Truth or Consequences

Objectives:

To consider appropriate school behaviors

To recognize the relationship between *behavior* and *consequence*

Time:

Two sessions

Materials:

Worksheet: "Can You Identify Behavior?"

Procedures:

1. Discuss dictionary definitions of terms: *behavior* and *consequences*.

2. Review difference between positive and negative consequences.

3. Distribute worksheet.

4. Read each situation aloud, discussing the behavior consequences, and whether the consequences are positive or negative.

5. Introduce the term *control,* eliciting a definition from the class.

6. Review the stories, asking students to tell whether or not the person could *control* the consequences.

Personal Application Discussion Questions

1. How much control do you have over the consequences of what you do at school?
2. How does it make you feel to know that you can/can't control the consequences?

Can You Identify Behavior?

In each of the boxed situations below, identify the behaviors with B, the consequences with C, and indicate if the consequences are positive (+) or negative (-).

1. Identify Mary's behavior and the consequences.

> *Mary is daydreaming in class. When the teacher calls on her, she does not know the answer— or even the question*

2. Identify Carlos' behavior and the consequences.

> *Carlos leans on a lamppost. All the lights in the city go out.*

3. Identify John's behavior and the consequences.

> *John's friends ask him to play ball after school. John turns them down because he has a project due in social studies the next day and he hasn't finished it.*

4. Identify *your* behavior and the consequences.

> *You had a fight with your best friend. You stay in the hall to get it settled, and you're late for class.*

5. Identify your behavior and the consequences.

> *Someone calls you a name on the playground. You walk away, but everyone there calls you "chicken."*

6. Identify Andy's behavior and the consequences.

> *Andy is in the boys' room. A friend is smoking in there and wants him to share the cigarette. Andy says, "No," but his friend says, "Aw, come on ..." Andy stays, smokes, and misses class.*

On the back of this sheet, write an example of your own that tells about one of *your* behaviors and the consequences.

A

Guess the Leader

Objective:

To help the group build a sense of community and *esprit de corps*.

Time:

One session

Procedures:

The group sits in a circle and one member is chosen to be "the detective." The detective goes out of the room and a leader is chosen. Then, when the detective comes back into the room all group members imitate the actions of the leader, while the detective tries to guess who is initiating the various motions or postures. For instance, the leader will casually cross his legs, others follow suit — but not in a mass movement. Then, the leader might scratch his ear or fold his hands. Others can then be designated a detectives and leaders in subsequent rounds.

Designing a Class Coat of Arms

Objective:

To build group identity by developing a personalized coat of arms.

Time:
One or two sessions

Materials:
Poster paper, felt pens,
masking tape

Procedures:

1. Prior to the start of this session, the advisor should draw a coat of arms on a large sheet of chart paper, dividing it into 6 roughly equal parts. Cut the coat of arms into six sections, marking the top of each section on the back.

2. Divide your total group into six task groups. Ask each group to choose a leader and send the leader to you.

3. Explain to the leaders that each group has a task to complete which will contribute to a total class project when put together. Randomly hand out one of the tasks on the following page to each leader. Tell them their time constraints, answer any questions, and give each leader a section of the coat of arms. (Modify the tasks to be more appropriate to your group if needed.)

4. Monitor the groups, offering encouragement, clarification, and an occasional idea or suggestion as they work on their task. Make sure their drawing is placed right side up.

5. Each leader reads the group's task to the class and shows the results. Carefully attach the chart paper to another larger piece of paper to display the final product.

6. You might allow some settling time and come back to the coat of arms on another day to refine and improve results.

*With modifications, this exercise can be used to develop a class banner, shield, or symbol.

A

DESIGNING A CLASS COAT OF ARMS (continued)

Task for Group One

Decide on appropriate class colors and put them into a design on your part of the coat of arms. Be prepared to tell the class why you chose those colors. (Example: *blue for loyalty, green for pride*)

Task for Group Two

Decide on a mascot that represents the class and then draw the mascot on your section of the coat of arms. Be prepared to tell why you chose the mascot. (Example: *elephant*, strong and intelligent)

Task for Group Three

Design a symbol that could represent the class and then draw the symbol on your section of the coat of arms. Be prepared to tell why you chose the symbol selected. (Example: *four leaf clover,* because we feel this will be a lucky group)

Task for Group Four

Decide on a wish you would like to grant your whole school and then draw a symbol that represents the wish on your section of the coat of arms. Be prepared to explain your wish and symbol to the class. (Example: our wish is for the winning attitude, and the symbol is a *male and female with hands raised in victory*)

Task for Group Five

Decide on a motto for the class and put the motto on your section of the coat of arms. Be prepared to explain your choice to the class. (Examples: *United we stand* is our motto and it represents the way we should tackle problems this year)

Task for Group Six

Decide on three words you hope people will remember this class for and then write these words on your section of the coat of arms. Be prepared to explain your choice to the class. (Example: *Caring, loyal* and *strong,* because we think that our class can live up to these values)

Goals and Goal Setting

Objective:

To help students set appropriate academic and personal goals

Time:

One to three sessions

Materials:

Three goal setting sheets (see next pages)

Procedures:

Follow directions on the worksheets provided

Goal Setting

List 3 negatives about your school work!

List 3 positives about your school work!

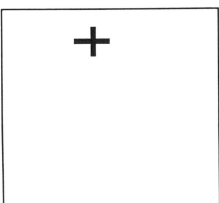

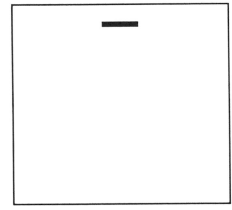

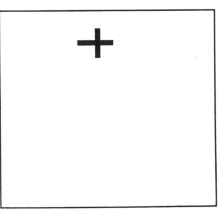

GOALS!

Using your positive statement on the first sheet,

      write *three* goals beginning each one with "I enjoy"

      or "I am" or "I take pride in ...".

      Example: "I take pride in completing

             all my assignments in ENGLISH."

Reinforce the positive.

1.

2.

3.

A Goal I Achieved

State a recent goal that you achieved that was important to you, and then answer the questions below.

My goal was to:

1. **What steps did you have to take to achieve your goal?**

2. **What was the hardest step?**

3. **How did you manage to achieve this hard step?**

4. **How did you feel when you achieved your goal?**

5. **Whom did you tell about it?**

B

How Did I Do?

Objective:

Provide a means for students to log goals achieved each day of a week

Time:
Two sessions

Materials:
"A Goal A Day" sheet

Procedures:

Every day for a week, list one goal you would like to accomplish that day. At the end of the day, or first thing the next morning, mark the degree in which you feel you achieved your goal throughout the week.

Closure:

Be prepared to discuss how you feel about your total week. Did the process of setting daily goals make you feel good or frustrated? Do you think the goals helped you accomplish things you might not have accomplished otherwise?

A Goal A Day

Goal	Not Achieved	Partially Achieved	Achieved
Monday			
Tuesday			
Wednesday			
Thursday			
Friday			

Constructing Relationships

Objective:

To have students discuss adolescence and the changes it brings so that they can have a better understanding of self.

Time:

One or more sessions

Materials:

Teacher copy of "Growing Patterns"
"Who Am I?" (handout)

Procedures:

1. Read to students "Growing Patterns" (teacher copy).

2. Discuss briefly the four teen situations.

3. Students complete individually the "Who Am I" handout.

C

GROWING PATTERNS

Adolescence is the period between childhood and adulthood. During these years your body, your thoughts, and your feelings go through changes. These changes reflect extensive growth: physical, mental, social, and emotional growth. These changes bring many problems you never knew as a child. Meeting and solving these problems are parts of becoming an adult.

In the years between 10 and 15, you discover new things about yourself. You may have new and different feelings about your friends. Friendships become more complex. You think and question more than you did when you were younger. Your body is developing in a new way.

Listen to these cases which we'll discuss.

"Being fourteen and over five foot ten, I was heads above everyone else. I couldn't feel normal. I worried that I would spend the rest of my life looking down at my friends. Now, you know, it doesn't seem to bother me at all. Being tall really helps when you play basketball."
▼▼▼▼▼▼▼▼

"In the seventh grade, everything started to go wrong. I wasn't interested in model airplanes anymore, and I wasn't ready to start dating. I wasn't sure where I was going. The toughest thing was not being able to concentrate on anything. The people around me got upset: my parents, my teachers, even my best friend. They were angry with me because I just didn't care about doing anything. I spent a lot of time watching TV. I felt bored."

▼▼▼▼▼▼▼▼▼

"Being a teenager was really tough for me. I had a bad case of acne, and I felt that people were always staring at my skin. I questioned everything people said, and I felt angry most of the time. Someone said I should join the debating club, and I did. I met a girl there, and we started to date. One day when my sister said she was glad to see me smiling, I realized I wasn't so angry anymore. Things have finally started to look up."
▼▼▼▼▼▼▼▼

"When I was ten, my body was already changing. Not one of my friends was changing; and, believe me, I felt like a freak! In a few months, though, a lot of my friends started going through the same thing. I felt better when I saw that they were changing, too."
▼▼▼▼▼▼▼▼

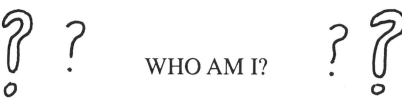

WHO AM I?

Which activities on this list do you prefer? Your choices are clues to your interests and abilities.

Part 1

DIRECTIONS: Circle the letter before the activity that you would prefer in each of the pairs below.

A. taking a math class ——————— C. taking an art class
B. working as a nurse's aide ——— E. working as a carpenter's assistant
E. building a doghouse——————— C. painting a poster
B. teaching a nursery school class—— D. planning a club project
A. running a cash register——————— B. helping someone with a problem
D. managing a school store——————— A. keeping records for a school team
A. being treasurer of a club——————— E. building a model car
C. writing a short story——————— D. directing a play
A. making a budget ——————— E. fixing a clock
B. playing a game with a team——— C. inventing a game

Part 2

DIRECTIONS: Count the number of times you chose each letter above, and write in your totals below.

_____ A. working with numbers _____ B. working with people _____ C. using creativity
_____ D. planning and managing _____ E. making and building

Part 3

DIRECTIONS: Think of times you have felt satisfied with an accomplishment. Fill in examples in the left-hand column of the chart below. In the right-hand column, classify each item on your list according to the categories given in Part 2.

	Examples	Classification (A, B, C, D, E)
1. something I created or made		_____
2. a game or hobby I enjoyed		_____
3. a compliment someone gave me		_____
4. something I am good at		_____
5. something I like to do in my free time		_____
6. my favorite subject in school		_____
7. something I would like to learn to do		_____

C

Deep Voice, String Bean, Oink Oink

Objective:
To help students become aware of problems common to middle school students and to begin developing problem-solving skills

Time:
One session

Procedures:

Discuss the following situations:

1. Danny Smith is twelve years old. He is very tall for his age, and his voice is beginning to get deeper. While giving a report in social studies class, his voice changed in the middle of an important passage. The class roared with laughter.

2. Jody Ann refused to get dressed for physical education class. She cried when approached by the teacher. After the counselor talked to Jody, she came back to the gym class and told the teacher that Jody was upset because several girls in class made fun of her string bean shape.

3. Timmy Johnson has been called into the principal's office for fighting. Normally Timmy is a quiet student, but during the last few days several students have been calling him *Fatso, Lard-bucket, Ten Ton Timmy,* and *Oink-Oink.*

Discussions should center around the following questions:

A.   What were the students' problems?

B.   Why do you think the students felt the way they did?

C.   How would you feel if you were one of these students?

D.   If you were one of these student's friends, what would you do?

E.   Do you have any problems like the problems in the three situations?

Wrap up: What other problems do middle school students feel awkward about?

C

Areas of Discomfort

Objective:
To help students recognize some of their characteristics that cause them discomfort

Time:
Two sessions

Materials:
"Areas of Discomfort" handout

Procedures:

1. Advisor discusses the developmental aspects of behavior for middle school students.

2. Students complete the "Areas of Discomfort" handout individually.

3. After they have done so, initiate discussion on such points as these:

   • Relate to individual differences.

   • Relate to the general characteristics of middle school students.

Note: File in folder so that this exercise could be repeated later in the year
          and comparisons made.

Areas of Discomfort

Directions: Read the list slowly, and as you come to a problem which bothers you, circle the number in front of it.

1. Being smaller than other kids.	23. Not enough time for fun and play.
2. Being bigger than other kids.	24. Hungry most of the time.
3. Can't talk plainly.	25. Not liking to eat.
4. Losing my temper.	26. Not being strong enough.
5. Having something wrong with me.	27. Being too fat.
6. Don't like school.	28. Being too thin.
7. Would like to join a school club.	29. Worrying.
8. Afraid of failing in school work.	30. Not smart enough.
9. Don't like art.	31. Don't like teachers.
10. Teachers always telling me what to do.	32. Not having any fun in school.
11. Too much work to do at home.	33. Not interested in books.
12. Nothing to do or play with at home.	34. Having to take music lessons.
13. Afraid of brother or sister.	35. Wanting adults at home more.
14. Not having my own room.	36. Adults won't help me.
15. Being too bashful.	37. Being made fun of.
16. Not knowing how to act at parties.	38. Playing mostly with little kids.
17. Kids not liking to play with me.	39. People think I'm a "sissy."
18. Never chosen as a leader.	40. Not able to work with others.
19. Being talked about.	41. Being watched all the time.
20. Afraid to try new things myself.	42. Not being able to sit still.
21. Can't forget mistakes I've made.	43. Having bad dreams.
22. Afraid of being punished.	44. Being careless.

C

This Is Me

Objective:

To help students identify how they perceive themselves

Time:

One session

Materials:

Worksheet

Procedures:

Have students complete the sentences on the worksheet.

Follow up with students sharing with the class as they are willing what they wrote, noting similarities and differences.

THIS IS ME

1. I am happiest when

2. I get angry when

3. I am frightened by

4. I feel love when

5. I feel sad about

6. I get excited when

7. I am bored when I

8. I am most proud of

9. I get satisfaction out of

10. I put trust in

11. I get "hung up" over

12. I feel safe when

13. I feel peaceful when

14. I feel hurt when

15. Things that make me happy are

16. I am annoyed when

17. When I'm by myself I like to

For Me?

Objective:

To assist students in developing an understanding of human uniqueness and its relationship to them

Time:

One session

Materials:

Ink pad, manilla paper, scissors, and 3x5 index cards

Procedures:

1. Discuss what it means to be unique. How is everybody special?
2. Give students manilla paper and allow them to cut the paper in any shape or form.
3. Have students individually make their thumbprint on the manilla paper, using the ink pad.
4. Using their imagination, the students should make a picture with the thumbprints.
5. Students then write, "I am unique because..."
6. Elicit discussion using lead questions below.

State the following: "You are unique. There has never been anyone like you and there will never be again." Discuss: "Is that good or bad? Do you agree? What are some implications of the statement?" Ask three or four people to summarize the sessions on uniqueness.

Follow up: Make a bulletin board display

Variation: Ask each student to make a thumbprint on a 3x5 card. Shuffle the cards. Tell each person to find his thumbprint. Give them three minutes and then say, "Now we will fingerprint your thumb again to see whether you were right." Discuss how they found their thumbprints.

D

Focusing On Our Strengths

Objective:
To help students focus on their positive qualities

Time:
One or two sessions

Materials:
Two handouts

Procedures:

Initiate discussion with such statements as the following.

> Most of us have been taught since childhood to be modest about our
> achievements and strengths. Seldom, if ever, have we been encouraged
> to verbalize our perceptions of our positive qualities. In addition, most of
> us have become habitually accustomed to putting ourselves down for our
> weaknesses rather than applauding our strong points. It is even more
> difficult to acknowledge our strengths when we seldom think about them.

Students need to be encouraged to recognize and think about their strengths. They also
need to have a clear understanding of the differences between bragging and acknowledging
their good points. ("Love thy neighbor *as* thyself") They need to understand the legitimacy
and even the necessity of self-appreciation. They need to realize that they, like everyone
else, are unique combinations of strong points and weak points and that some weaknesses
can be overcome by hard work, while others must simply be accepted. They will appreciate
the good qualities they possess. By being urged to notice positive things about themselves —
whether or not they get approval from others — they will begin to learn the art of self-respect.

MY STRENGTHS

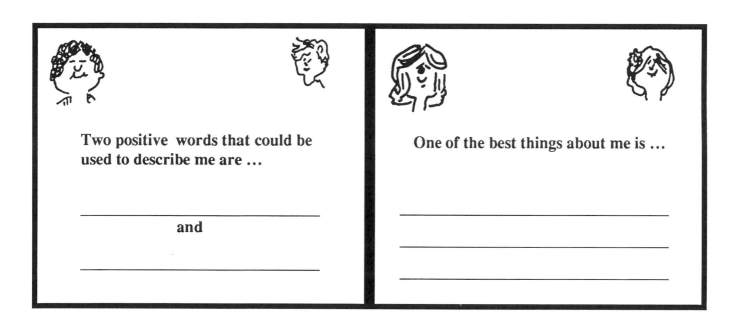

Two positive words that could be used to describe me are ...

_____

and

_____

One of the best things about me is ...

_____

_____

_____

I am good at ..._____

_____

_____

What is something good your friend might say about you?

_____

_____

_____

Times I've deserved a pat on the back

It is up to us to give ourselves recognition. If we wait for it to come from others, we feel resentful when it doesn't, and when it does, we may not believe it. It is not what others say to us that counts. We all love praise, but have you ever noticed how quickly the glow from a compliment wears off? When we compliment ourselves, the glow stays with us. It is still good to hear it from others, but it doesn't matter so much if we have already heard it from ourselves.

Take a look at the statements below. You've probably done each of these things at one time or another but have forgotten about it. (We tend to remember our failures and forget our strengths). Choose 4 of the 8 statements and describe a time you did each of those four things.

1. I tried something I thought would be difficult.

2. I avoided putting someone down even though I felt like it.

3. I stuck with a job that was hard to do and I finally finished it.

4. I avoided making excuses or blaming someone else for what I did.

5. I told the truth even though I was afraid I'd get in trouble.

6. I didn't go along with what others were doing because I thought it was wrong.

7. I controlled my temper in a difficult situation.

8. I tried to get along better with someone in my family.

Graffiti Mural

Objective:

To provide an opportunity for students to express their ideas freely on a variety of topics

Time:

One session

Materials:

Newsprint paper or tag board, colored markers

Procedures:

A graffiti mural is a non-threatening way for students to express their ideas and feelings. It also allows them to expand on the ideas of other students. A large piece of paper placed in a section of a chalkboard or wall can be used for the mural. A table can also be used by covering it with paper. Put a sentence starter or "title" at the top of the mural. For example:

"School is…"
"Students are…"
"Friendship is…"
"Teachers are…"
"To improve this classroom, I would like for our class to have…"
"It's tough being a kid because…"

You may need to provide encouragement for students to express themselves freely. You might wish to express your "teacher opinion" when the mural is underway. A few basic ground rules might be: (1) everyone contributes at least once, (2) nothing may be written that makes fun of another person.

After students have contributed hold a class discussion on the topic of the mural.

I would like our class to have:

a drinking fountain

A candy machine

A rug to sit on

A couch, so I can be more comfortable

A rocking chair

D

Group Action: Likes and Dislikes

Objective:
To demonstrate to students the variety of beliefs and values held by others

Time:
One or two sessions

Procedures:

1. As the adviser or one of the students calls out each item on the following two pages, students show how they feel about that item by: waving their hand high if it is very important (or true) for them; raising their hand halfway if it is fairly important; holding their hands down if the item is fairly unimportant (or untrue) to them.

    Have them move rapidly, and do not stop to discuss items until they are finished. Students are to vote on every item and for all parts of multiple response items as the leader calls them out.

2. Have someone record votes on the chalkboard or a piece of paper.

3. After all have voted the group might want to talk or write about some of the items.

4. Another day — with the entire class or in small groups — have them rank the items below in the order most important to them and discuss their reasons. You can have more discussion in small groups, although fewer people will hear each person. You might take more than one period for this.

    A. If if were some kind of "star" I would rather be: (a) a great doctor, (b) a movie star, (c) a famous scientist like Albert Einstein, (d) a famous writer, or (e) _____.

    B. If I could make one great contribution to the world, I would like: (a) to discover a cure for cancer, (b) stop all wars, (c) give everyone in the world enough food to keep healthy, or (d) _____.

D

ITEMS FOR VOTING:

1. Ice cream is one of the world's best desserts.

2. I have to get eight hours sleep every night to feel good.

3. I think everyone should learn to play at least one sport well.

4. People should always smile and appear friendly when they meet someone new.

5. The school cafeteria food is great!

6. All bombs and nuclear weapons should be banned from the world.

7. If I had a friend with bad breath, I would:
   a. tell him about it in a kind way
   b. say nothing, but try to avoid my friend.
   d. say nothing, do nothing, and hope for the best.

8. I believe people are happier if they stay with their own race.

9. I brush my teeth at least twice a day because:
   a. I want to have healthy teeth and gums
   b. my parents taught me to.
   c. I'm afraid no one will like me if I don't
   d. I don't brush my teeth twice a day!

10. I usually choose my own clothes.

11. I will argue, or even fight for what I believe.

12. At sometime in my life, I have stolen something.

13. I would be angry if someone told me to go away and leave him/her alone.

14. I eat vegetables every chance I get.

15. I like to work and to earn money.

16. I usually share whatever I have with other people.

17. I hate a sloppy eater!

18. If I saw an old man loaded down with packages trying to open a door, I would:
   a. open the door because it is good manners
   b. open the door because he obviously needs help
   c. let him get in the best way he can; it's not my problem.

(continued)

D

ITEMS FOR VOTING (continued)

19. I want to make good grades.

20. I want to make a lot of money.

21. I want to go to college.

22. I spend my money as soon as I get it.

23. I keep a journal or diary.

24. When I grow up I'll probably smoke cigarettes.

25. I think people should try as many drugs as they can, before deciding whether drugs are good or bad.

26. I already know what kind of job I want when I grow up.

27. If my country were at war, I would:
    a. fight, if I had to
    b. volunteer for fighting or any other service I could give
    c. not fight under any circumstances.

28. I like school

29. If, at a dinner party, I spilled my drink, I would:
    a. leave the table, feeling embarrassed
    b. quietly ask the hostess or a waiter for help
    c. cover the mess with my napkin and ignore it.

30. I like learning.

31. I often think of being someone else.

32. Learning about myself means a lot to me.

33. I like me.

How Much Do You Know About Self-Esteem?

Objective:

To provide an opportunity for students to think about self-esteem

Time:

One or two sessions

Materials:

Questionnaire:
"How Much Do You Know About Self-esteem?"

Procedures:

As every teacher knows, one way to teach information is to give students a test on it and then discuss the items as you correct them. This true/false test offers an opportunity for students to ponder statements about attitudes, beliefs, and behaviors related to self-esteem.

It is best to give the test by reading each item aloud to students as they read it and going slow enough for students to have a chance to think about the question. Every now and then, after reading aquestion ask: "Is that a true statement?" or "Do you agree or disagree?" Ask students not to express their opinions orally during the test, explaining that you'll be discussing items after the test.

An answer key has been provided which is based on consensus in the literature regarding the psychology of self-esteem. It is important, however, to make it clear to students that all answers are open to discussion and to encourage students to express their opinions. Listening to and challenging one another's statements leads many students to review their own experiences and opinions and to reconcile these new ideas.

The following are some general thoughts on self-esteem that may be useful to you and may become part of a discussion with your students:

Self-esteem begins to form at a very early age. Parents are the most powerful individuals who shape a child's self-esteem because of the amount of time they spend together and the child's total dependency upon them. Paradoxically, our concept of our self does not develop from the inside out, but rather is fashioned from the outside in. It is how we think we appear to others and how others judge us, that is largely responsible for how we view ourselves. Because we internalize the standards and opinions imposed on us by others, we tend to take on their attitudes and measure our own behavior in the way we think they would.

D

Our thoughts or beliefs about ourselves determine our behavior. Our judgment of ourselves influences the kinds of friends we choose, how we get along with others, and how productive we will be. It affects our creativity, integrity, stability, and whether we will be a leader or a follower. Our feelings of self-worth form the core of our personality and determine the use we make of our aptitudes and abilities. Our attitude toward ourselves has a direct bearing on how we live all parts of our life.

Feelings of being inadequate or inferior are among the most pervasive and destructive human emotions. Many people discredit themselves, focusing on their shortcomings and ignoring or discounting their good qualities.

It is true that there are people who seem blissfully unaware of their faults and project faults on others. Positive self-esteem, however, is not to be confused with self-centeredness, being a braggart, or acting superior, all of which are attempts to hide negative feelings about self.

One of the ways for students to develop positive self-esteem is to acquire an awareness of their personal uniqueness. Each student needs to know and feel that he or she is somehow special, one of a kind, and can never be duplicated. The likelihood of any one person ever being genetically like another is 102,400,000,000 to one. Each person contributes to the world in a unique way.

Another way for students to develop positive self-esteem is to develop realistic beliefs about mistakes and failures, performance and accomplishments. They need to realize that mistakes are a general human condition and that they are not less valuable and lovable because they fail or make mistakes. They need to see that they, as persons, are separate from their behavior and that their value does not depend on their performance or accomplishments.

Finally, students need to understand the phenomenon of self-criticism or critical inner speech and realize that they have a choice regarding their own worth. They need to consistently give themselves private "support-talks" and focus on their strengths rather than their deficiencies.

Answer Key:	1. T,	2. T,	3. F,	4. T,	5. F,	6. T,	7. T,	8. T,	9. F,	10. T,
	11. F,	12. T,	13. T,	14. T,	15. F,	16. T,	17. F,	18. T,	19. T,	20. T,
	21. T,	22. T,	23. T,	24. F,	25. T,	26. T,	27. T,	28. F,	29. F,	30. T,

How Much Do You Know About Self-esteem?

T F   1. How you feel about yourself affects everything you do in life.

T F   2. People respond positively to people who like themselves.

T F   3. Most people think they're great.

T F   4. By the way a baby is treated it learns to feel like a worthwhile person or not a worthwhile person.

T F   5. People who are intelligent or good looking almost always have high self-esteem.

T F   6. If you like yourself, others will like you too.

T F   7. If a person is told frequently that he/she is incapable of doing something, that person probably believes that he/she can't do it.

T F   8. Once a person believes he/she is worthwhile, he/she no longer needs to present a false front to others.

T F   9. The feelings others have about us never become our feelings about ourselves.

T F 10. People can learn to like themselves even if they think others don't like them.

T F 11. It's possible to get everyone to like you.

T F 12. We become what we think we are.

T F 13. You don't have to be perfect to be worthwhile. You only have to be yourself.

T F 14. Some people who are afraid of failure don't try.

T F 15. The only way to truly like yourself is to be perfect at the things that are important to you.

T F 16. People try hard to avoid making mistakes but no one succeeds.

T F 17. Of the billions of people in the world, there are only a few exactly like you.

T F 18. Neither your accomplishments nor your looks add anything to your true, basic worth.

T F 19. Feeling like a rotten person does not prove you are rotten, merely that you think you are.

T F 20. Being different from everyone else in the world makes you special.

T F 21. People who brag about their accomplishments often have very low self-esteem.

T F 22. There is no such thing as a worthless human being.

T F 23. Everyone has some things to be proud of.

T F 24. Having good feelings about yourself means you're conceited.

T F 25. Each person has talents and abilities just waiting to be discovered.

T F 26. "Once a failure, always a failure" is false.

T F 27. Your mind is like a tape recorder, taping what people say to you about yourself and then playing it back to you.

T F 28. Trying to talk to yourself in a kind way is silly.

T F 29. What you say to yourself about your own worth never determines how you feel about yourself.

T F 30. If you tell yourself you are going to fail at something, you're more likely to fail.

For each question you got wrong, subtract 3 points from 100

100

−   (3 x each wrong answer)

_____

Total score

D

IALAC ("I Am Lovable and Capable")

Objectives:
To help students recognize the things we do and say to one another which affect our self-esteem
To begin building a commitment to establish a supportive classroom climate

Time:
Two sessions

Materials:
A piece of paper with letters IALAC written on it.
IALAC story/chalkboard/chalk

Background Information:

The "I Am Lovable and Capable" (IALAC) story provides a simple but powerful learning experience in how we influence, positively and negatively, each other's self-esteem. It was originally developed by Sidney Simon and is "required reading" for anyone who works with people.

The idea behind IALAC is that each of us wears a sign saying "I Am Lovable and Capable," except the signs are invisible, so people frequently forget they are there. During the course of a day, people say things to us and do things to us that tend to build up our signs, making us feel more lovable or more capable, or tear down our signs, leaving us feeling less lovable or less capable. Some people feel and act pretty lovable but not so capable, or quite capable but not so lovable. Actually, no one is all one way or the other. We all feel lovable and capable in some areas and situations and not so lovable or capable in others. But people who do feel more lovable and capable tend to both accomplish more and have more satisfying relationships.

How we get along in life is in good measure determined by how people treated our IALAC signs when we were younger. As we get older, we become less vulnerable to being influenced by what people say and do to us. We can process incoming stimuli differently and make better sense out of it. But most of us are still somewhat vulnerable, no matter how independent we may be. The area of "self-concept" and "self-esteem" in psychology can be related to the notion of the IALAC sign we all wear. By telling the IALAC story to students, we share part of this important concept with the whole class. This increases everyone's sensitivity to the feelings of others. It is very difficult to tear down someone else's IALAC sign when we are aware that that is what we are doing. And it is much more likely that we will help build up one another's sign if we become aware of how important those signs are.

We recommend that you read Simon's IALAC story yourself and then tell the students the IALAC story in your own words, creating examples and anecdotes of your own to illustrate the many ways an IALAC sign can be ripped in a single day. We have provided a version of this story below. But remember, the main character can be male or female, young or old, black or white, teacher or student, or whatever, and the anecdotes within the story can be changed with the point of the story remaining exactly the same.

D

Procedures:

Part I

To begin this session, you might simply say, "Yesterday we explored some issues related to the question of 'What makes a safe environment for learning?' Today I would like to share with you a story that might give us further insights about that question." Then, proceed to tell the story.

When telling the story, actually wear a sign labelled "IALAC." You can simply write it on a piece of paper and tape it to your shirt or dress. Whenever you get to a part of the story where a piece of the IALAC sign is torn, you show this by actually ripping a piece of your IALAC sign.

After you have told the story, have the students get into pairs with someone they do not know or do not know well. Give each pair five to ten minutes to do the following:

    (1)   Share with each other one time in the past month when someone ripped a piece of their IALAC sign and one time in the past month when someone added a piece to their IALAC sign."

    (2)   Together, come up with a list of "Five ways people rip one another's IALAC signs in our school or community."

Part II

Now, have the group come together so that everyone can see the large piece of newsprint you have placed on the wall. Ask someone to come up and stand right against the piece of newsprint and have someone else use a crayon or marker to trace a full-scale outline of the person's body on the newsprint. Once the person steps away from the wall, a large tracing of the outline of a human body will be left behind.

Explain to the class: As you no doubt realized in your pairs, one of the most effective ways that we tear down each other's IALAC signs is through the use of put-downs, digs, "killer statements," or whatever you want to call them. There is no more sure way of preventing a class from being a safe place where people grow together than by having lots of killer statements in the air most of the time. I hope we can make this classroom one that's free of killer statements. That doesn't mean we won't have any humor or fun together — just not humor that is at someone else's expense. So, I'd like us to do a short symbolic ritual here by having this outline of a human body receive all the put-downs and killer statements which might have been said in this group if we allowed them. There are several markers up front here, so just come on up and write down all the digs, rotten names, and put-downs you can think of.

Leave off the swear words, though; I know we can think of plenty of others without those. Here, I'll start it off with this one, "you idiot!"

A second way of accomplishing this task would be to have one volunteer do the writing while the other students call out all the killer statements they've heard in school.

Allow enough time for everyone who wants to come up and write a killer statement on the figure. Most likely it will be filled up with quite a collection of unpleasant words and phrases. Then fold or roll up the sheet of newsprint and put it away in a drawer, closet or shelf, saying something like, "You know from the movies how cowboys or sheriffs, when entering their homes, hang their gun belts on a hook by the door. It was their way of saying here is one place we can come to without having to defend ourselves every minute, where we can just relax and enjoy ourselves.. Well, that's what I hope our group can develop — a place where we hang our killer statements on the wall and not have to defend ourselves against others who might rip our IALAC signs to shreds."

Taking the time to build a foundation of trust like this goes a long way. It can mean the difference between a successful and unsuccessful class. It's no guarantee against some put-downs occurring, but it would be unlikely for them to get out of hand, and an occasional "Ouch, that tore my IALAC sign" may be enough to have everyone remember how destructive comments like that can be.

Assignment

Before the group breaks up, give this brief homework assignment to everyone. "Bring in some item that is important to you — that symbolizes something you like to do or that represents you in some way. It could be a record, a helmet, a poem, a picture or whatever. You will be asked to show it to others and explain its meaning to you; so don't bring in anything you'd rather not talk about."

A SAMPLE IALAC STORY

Chip wakes up one morning and the first words he hears are his mother yelling, "Hurry up, or you'll be late for school!" (rip). He darts down the hall to the bathroom but his sister beats him to it and slams the door in his face (rip). When he finally gets in, he sees that she forgot to take his gym shorts off the shower curtain rod, and they are now soaked from his sister's shower (rip).

On the way to school, he walks past a group of girls he knows, one of whom he has had his eye on for quite a while. As he passes by, he sees her point his way and all her friends start whispering (rip). Later on, he sees a little boy who fell and skinned his knee. He helps him up, collects his books that are strewn over the sidewalk, and gives him a word of encouragement. The boy says, "Thanks a lot, mister" (add a piece back on). But helping the boy makes him just a half minute late for school. Since it's not the first time he's been late, the homeroom teacher sends him down to the office. He tries to explain about the little boy who fell. "Likely story," and he gets detention (rip).

His first class that morning is English. He gets back a spelling test from the week before (big rip). In math he gets called on and gives the wrong answer (rip). In music class, the teacher suggests that maybe it would be better if he just mouthed the words (rip). During lunch, while he is trying to get up enough nerve to ask Jennifer, the girl from this morning's whispering, to a rock concert, his best friend Jeff comes up to him and tells him that he and Jennifer are going to the concert (start to rip a piece, but don't tear it all the way off)... but then he thinks to himself, "Oh well, there's another concert in two weeks. I'll ask Jennifer earlier this time, and if she says no, I'd also like to go with Betty. I'll ask her." (Drop you hand off the piece you were tearing, leaving it partly intact.)

He has supper early because tonight is the first game his B-string basketball team is playing that season. When he gets out on the court, he sees that both his parents are in the stands. He didn't

D

expect that, since they are usually too busy to come to his games (add a piece back on). Unexpectedly, the coach puts him in the starting line-up (add a piece back on). He plays an average game most of the night, but misses both foul shots (rip). He hears his father say sarcastically, "My son, the athlete" (rip). Mary comes up to him, puts her hand on his arm and says, "Nice try, Chip" and smiles at him like she really means it (add a piece back on). On the way home he hears the local newscaster announce, "The Northside Rockets lost their first game tonight when Chip Jackson missed two shots at the free throw line…"(rip).

When he gets home, Mom and Dad have had time to discuss his report card which came in the mail from school that day. They inform him he got two Cs. His mother says, "Why can't you be like your sister, she got all Bs and an A this time" (rip). His father says, "You'd better set your clock tonight. With your grades you can't afford to be late to school" (rip). He goes up to his room, where the family's golden retriever comes trotting in and puts his head down on Chip's lap (add a piece).

Chip takes his IALAC sign off (take your sign off) puts it at the side of the bed, pulls the covers up over himself, and drifts off to sleep.

Hurt City — I.A.L.A.C. — Bulletin Boards

Objective:
To provide practice in expressing feelings in a non-threatening way

Time:
Ongoing activity

Materials:
Two large pieces of
butcher or comparable paper

Procedures:

1. Advisor will post butcher paper on wall. Label one HURT CITY and the other I.A.L.A.C.

2. Explain to the group they may write on either paper to express the good and bad things which happen to them. Good comments (such as, "I passed my test," "I got a compliment on my hair." etc.) go to the I.A.L.A.C. paper. Negative comments ("I broke up with my girlfriend," "I got a D on my report," etc.) go on the HURT CITY paper.

3. Students do not have to sign statements.

4. Leave the boards up for two or three weeks; occasionally note with the group the number of positive statements as opposed to negative.

D

The Me I Want To Be
and How I Can Get There

Objective:

To involve the students in committing to a self-improvement goal.

Time:

One session initially
   with a second one later

Materials:

Student handouts:
   "The Me I Want To Be and How I Can Get There"
   "Put Your Self-Respect First"

Procedures:

The questions on the handouts are designed to lead students to focus on one behavior that, if changed, would result in them liking themselves better. You may ask students to fold their paper and staple it and give it to you and tell them you'll give them back to them in a week and they can then evaluate their progress.

Once a failure
Always a failure

A MYTH TO QUIT BELIEVING

THE ME I WANT TO BE AND HOW I CAN GET THERE

When do you like yourself most?
    Remember some time when you felt really great, when you were glad to be you.
    Describe the times and the circumstances.

What could you do to feel this way again?

What are some things you could do that would make you like yourself better?

Choose one thing and make it a goal:

Develop a step by step plan of what you will have to do to reach your goal.

Personal Plan:

Put Your Self-Respect First

If everyone thinks the same things are important for you to do and you agree with them, you're lucky. If you are like most kids, different people in your life have different ideas about what you should do. Think about the different behaviors people want from you and write them below.

I would be successful in my parents' eyes if I	I would be successful in my teachers' eyes if I	I would be successful my friends'eyes if I if I	I would be successful in my own eyes if I
_____	_____	_____	_____
_____	_____	_____	_____
_____	_____	_____	_____

Some kids think they are failures if they don't live up to everyone's expectations. Some drive themselves their entire lives trying to get everyone's approval so that they will feel that they are worthwhile. They dread being told that they are not okay so they keep telling themselves one or more of the following:

TRY HARDER — "If I just work harder, I'll be okay."
BE PERFECT — "If I am just perfect, I'll be okay."
PLEASE OTHERS — "If I just please everyone, I'll be okay."
BE STRONG — "If I just don't show my feelings, I'll be okay."
HURRY UP — "If I just do more things faster, I'll be okay."
Trying to base your self-esteem on the respect and approval of others is an exhausting task. Even when you deserve it you don't always get it. The most important way to maintain self-esteem is to do those things that will cause you to respect and approve of *yourself*. Try to think of something that *you* think you should do — one thing that you'd respect yourself for doing. Maybe it's getting up 15 minutes earlier in the morning, not putting off your homework in the evening, organizing your notebook, not putting someone down, etc. Write it here: I would respect myself a lot if I

Think about how you would feel if you did the behavior you just described. I would feel

Think about how you would feel if you didn't do it. I would feel

If you sense you would be a little disappointed or disgusted with yourself, then why not decide to do it today? Nothing raises self-respect like a little ACTION!

Tips For Better Listening

Objective:
To have students learn the importance of good listening skills.

Time: **Materials:**
One or two sessions   Paper/pencil

Procedures:

1. Begin by saying: In just a minute you are going to get some directions. It will be an exercise to see how good a listener you are. You will need a sheet of paper and a pencil. (Have students get that out now so they will be ready.)

It will also be important that you know the meanings of the words *parallel* and *vertical*. Draw lines on board to illustrate meanings of both words.)

When the directions start, you are to listen carefully — do not talk. Concentrate on your own paper and do your very best listening.

2. Say: a. Locate the upper left-hand corner of your paper.
            b. Without making a mark, move your pencil down the left-hand side of the page about two inches.
            c. From that point move to the right two inches and make a dot.
            d. From that dot, draw a one-inch line to the right and parallel with the top of the page.

3. At this point, say: "Now stop. Just in case you're feeling totally confused, I'm going to give you a chance to start over. Turn your papers over and I'll begin again. But no more second changces." (Read again all that is above and then continue through to the end without any more pauses.)

            e. Move back to the dot and draw a five-inch line parallel with the left hand side of the paper and towards the bottom of your paper.

            f. From the bottom end of this line, draw another line three inches long to the right and parallel to the bottom of your paper.

E

    g.   From the end of this line, draw a one-inch line up and parallel to the right-hand side of the paper.

    h.   From the end of this line, going towards the left, draw a line two inches long parallel to the bottom of the page.

    i.   Draw a vertical line from this point, joining with the right end of the first line you drew.

    j.   Check your paper. You should have drawn the letter "L."

4. Discuss:

    a.   What kinds of things do you like to listen to? Why? (Probably stories, TV, music, things that are fun, interesting, exciting, etc., things that involve emotions.)

    b.   What kinds of things do you not like to listen to? Why? (Probably … social studies reports, speeches, directions, etc., informational types of activities.

    c.   How is listening for information different from listening for entertainment? (More concentration and closer attention are necessary when one is listening for information.)

5.   Students might be interested to know that one of the reasons our minds tend to wander when we're really trying to listen is the difference in the rate a person talks and the rate at which we can think. Normal speech is generally between 150-200 words per minute. The mind is actually able to think at speeds up to a thousand words per minute. Therefore, if we are not making an effort to think about what the speaker is saying, our minds will begin to think about something else.

6. Discuss: What are some things to remember about good listening?

    Be ready to listen when the speaker begins to talk. This is not the time to be cleaning off your desk, combing your hair, looking for a pen/pencil. Be ready to listen carefully to what is said.

7. If interest warrants it, a second effort to construct a more complicated letter, such as H or A, could be included.

Magic Keys To Good Listening

Objective:
To assist students in becoming aware of good listening skills.

Time:
One session

Materials:
Transparency of the three
"Magic Keys to Good Listening"
(if necessary could be a handout)

Procedures:

Place students in groups of threes. Two students will take turns speaking for two minutes each. Third person is the observer who will be critiquing the two students communicating. The observer is asked to comment on the three guidelines listed. Students could be asked to discuss a time they got in trouble with parents, school, etc.

In the "Magic Keys" sheet the teacher can use the following discussion questions:

1.   What are some reasons why you did that?
2.   How did you feel afterward?
3.   If you could do it over, how would you do it differently?
4.   How did (or would) it make her/him feel?
5.   What is it that makes it difficult, fun, exciting, etc.?
6.   How would you do it?
7.   What do you think would happen if you did that?
8.   What help do you need?
9.   Would you feel good about yourself?
10. What do you like most about it? Least?
11. What bothers you about that?
12. How would you improve it?
13. Are you saying that _____?
14. Could you say a bit more about that?

Magic Keys To Good Listening

A. FOCUSING.

- Give the person who is speaking the center of attention.

- Maintain eye contact with the speaker.

- Do not interrupt, tell your own stories, or give your opinions without being asked.

B. ACCEPTING.

- Nod. smile! Show that you understand.

- You may not always agree with the speaker, but listen with interest and respect.

C. DRAWING OUT.

- By asking good questions, the speaker will feel free to express himself, and you'll learn more about people and the topic.

Did You Get All Of That?

Objective:
To help students become aware of the part that memory plays in good listening

Time:
One session

Materials:
Paper/pencil

Procedures:

1. Read the following situations slowly but without repeating and allow students to test themselves in their ability to recall the necessary information.

    a. For a free copy of Mr. Harris' talk, send your name and address to Educational Services, General Motors Corporation, Box 364, Detroit, Michigan 78965.
        > What is the box number?
        > What will you get?
        > What city do you send to?
        > What was the zip code given?

    b. A sample lesson will show you how pleasant and profitable it can be to study radio engineering at home. Send for free lessons now. No cost to you. No obligation. Write tonight to American School of Radio Engineering, 790 Commonwealth Avenue, Boston, Massachusetts 02215.
        > What is being offered?
        > What is the name of the school?
        > What is the street number?
        > How much does it cost?
        > Did you get all of that?

    c. When you hear the air-raid warning, follow these directions. Pull over to the side of the road. Leave lanes open for emergency vehicles. Shut off motor and lights. Open windows. Get out and go to a shelter if one is available; if not, crouch down in the car. Resume travel only when the all-clear sounds. For official civilian defense instructions, tune to the designated emergency broadcast radio station.
        > Should you remain in your car?
        > Should you open or close your windows?
        > Which lane should you stay in?
        > Should you turn off the car lights?
        > What radio station should you listen to?

E

d. Because tomorrow's assembly is scheduled for fourth period, girls in sections 3-G, 3-K, and 3-M will eat during the second lunch period. Boys in these sections will report to the assembly hall at the end of the first lunch period.

> Which students are to have second lunch?
> When should girls report?
> Where should the boys go?
> When should they go?

e. Walk east on Common Street for two blocks until you come to Lynch's Drugstore. Turn right and continue on Madison Street. Number 264 Madison Street is the third house from the corner of Madison and Common Streets.

> How many blocks must you walk before you reach the drugstore?
> How many houses from the corner is the one you want?
> What is the number of the house?
> What is the names of the drugstore?

2. Check answers and discuss how memory and interest affect the quality of our listening.

Say What?

Objective:
To increase students' ability to listen objectively and paraphrase a speaker's comments

Time:
One session

Procedures:

One person in the group is designated the speaker. The individual will speak briefly on a chosen topic. When finished, the person next to the speaker must paraphrase correctly what the first person said before he/she gets his/her own chance to speak.

Suggested topics:
My favorite person.
The best or worst thing about this school.
What I think about ...

        war
        drugs
        abortion
        gun laws
        hobbies
        school rules
        government

Any topic that requires a student to explain his/her position will suffice.

Additional suggestions:
1. Put a time limit of one minute for the speaker to state his/her position.
2. Students could all speak to the same topic, could select a topic of their choice, or could randomly select a topic.
3. Rather than the person on the side of the speaker paraphrasing, any person could be randomly selected to paraphrase.

When completed, ask the following questions:

1. What must be done if you are going to paraphrase someone?
2. Which is easier: talking for yourself or paraphrasing what someone else said?
3. Were you more careful of what you were going to say because you knew someone was going to repeat what you said?

E

My Listening Skills

Objective:
To enable students to evaluate their own listening skills

Time:
One session

Materials:
Handout

Procedures:

Distribute "My Listening Skills" handouts to students. Ask them to look at the list and check anything they feel is true for them. In groups of two have them compare their answers and discuss the *where, when,* and *why* they behaved in that way. They can also discuss what it feels like to converse with someone who does not do any of the things listed.

MY LISTENING SKILLS

_____ 1. Told another person what I like about him/her.

_____ 2. Maintained eye contact.

_____ 3. Paid full attention to other's thoughts and words.

_____ 4. Helped someone else join the discussion.

_____ 5. Helped someone to share his/her feelings openly.

_____ 6. Gave a helpful suggestion after asking permission.

_____ 7. Found a positive way to handle a negative situation.

_____ 8. Asked another person or group for help.

_____ 9. Explained my own ideas clearly, without putting others down.

_____ 10. Did not force my own opinions on the person speaking.

_____ 11. Tried not to take up all of the group's time.

E

I Heard It Through The Grapevine

Objective:

To provide practice in listening carefully and passing on information correctly.

Time:

One session

Materials:

Message cards

Procedures:

Five students are arranged in a circle or line. The leader starts with a message which is whispered to #1 and then whispered to each successive student. The fifth (or final student) repeats what he/she heard and this is compared with the original.

Variation 1

Prepare a message card which can be compared visually by the total group when the grapevine is completed.

Variation 2

Five students are selected as participants and four of these students leave the room and wait in the hall. The student who has remained in the room (#1) is read a message from a printed card. Student #2 is then called back into the room, and student #1 repeats the message, without being able to see the printed card. Student #3 is then called back into the room and student #2 must then tell him/her the message. The activity proceeds in this manner until student #5 has received the message and repeated what he/she has heard. The advantage of this method is that the rest of the class can hear how the message changes as it is relayed by the participants.

Sample Messages

1. I'm having a birthday party at my house on Thursday, January 27, at 4:00 p.m.
2. My telephone number is 473-5968.
3. John Smith lives at 325 Wabash Avenue, Apartment #12.
4. Three of the best movies ever made are *Mary Poppins, The Sound of Music,* and *Charlotte's Web.*
5. Mt. St. Helens erupted violently on May 18, 1980.
6. Edmonds School District No. 15 has many school buses.

Discuss with the group the factors that caused the message to end up differently from the original and what helped the message to be successfully repeated each time?

Active Listening

Objective:
To provide students with the opportunity to assess their own feelings.

Time:
One session

Materials:
Pencil/pen, paper
Active Listening Worksheet & Key

Procedures:

1. Hand out worksheet and ask students to complete individually.
2. Divide the class into groups of four or five. In these groups students share and compare their individual responses and try to arrive at a consensus response for each of the given comments.
3. When students finish, distribute the key of suggested answers.
4. Hold a discussion among the entire class in which you present the idea of active listening.
5. Follow up the discussion of active listening in one or both of the following ways.

   a. Have students choose one of the situations on the worksheet or create one of their own and write a dialogue in which one person actively listens to the other. Then have them evaluate each other's dialogues by placing the appropriate codes used in the key next to each statement by the active listener. Effective dialogues are coded with mostly U's.
   b. Have students choose one of the situations on the worksheet and, in pairs, role play the persons involved. One student is to role play the person with the problem. The other is to use active listening. Students can tape their role-plays and code the tape-recorded conversation as above.

6. To bring closure discuss such questions as the following:

   a. How could knowing how to be an active listener be useful to you on a job?
   b. What are some occasions when active listening would not be appropriate?

Active Listening Worksheet

Instructions

Read each of the following comments and circle the number of the response below it which comes closest to what you think you would say to this person. Then check the key to see what type of a response you chose.

Comment 1

Why do some people talk all the time in class when they have nothing to say? It makes me angry. I wish they would just shut up! They're only trying to impress the teacher.

1. You really shouldn't be too critical of others. What is apparent to you might not be apparent to them.
2. You think some people talk in class to win points with the teacher.
3. I get pretty dismayed by some of the things people say in class, too.
4. You think some people talk unproductively in class and it makes you angry.
5. Do you also get the impression that a lot of this kind of business goes on after class around the teacher's desk?

Comment 2

I always seem to do the wrong thing. I'm just a jerk.

1. You feel like the worst person in the whole world.
2. How long have you felt this way?
3. You feel you never do anything right.
4. I feel that way sometimes, too.
5. You should know better than to run yourself down. You'll never get anywhere that way.

Comment 3

Just leave me alone! I don't want to talk with anyone or do anything. No one cares about me.

1. I felt just like that one time.
2. That's a stupid thing to say.
3. You're upset and you don't want to talk with anyone because you feel no one cares.
4. Has someone hurt you badly?
5. You feel like people hate you.

Comment 4

I don't want to play with Jim anymore. He's a dummy, and he's selfish and mean.

1. You are threatened by him so you don't want to play with him anymore.
2. It isn't nice to call someone a dummy.
3. You're angry with Jim because you feel he is selfish and mean.
4. I know how you feel.
5. What did you do to him?

KEY TO ACTIVE LISTENING

Comment 1	Comment 2	Comment 3	Comment 4
1. E	1. I	1. S	1. I
2. I	2. P	2. E	2. E
3. S	3. U	3. U	3. U
4. U	4. S	4. P	4. S
5. P	5. E	5. I	5. P

E = Evaluative: A remark that classifies and places some kind of label on a statement

S = Supportive: A remark which says "I agree with you" or "I feel that way too."

I = Interpretive: A response that goes beyond what is included in the original remark. It attempts to place the speaker in a position he/she may not feel he/she belongs in.

P = Probing: A response which attempts to find the reasons for the original remarks.

U = Understanding: A response which reflects back to the speaker what was said and/or what was felt and indicates that the listener understands and accepts the information conveyed without evaluating or labeling it.

F

Killer Statements Hurt

Objectives:

To become aware of the concept of Killer Statements and to be able to identify them in everyday conversations.

Time:
One or two sessions

Materials:
Pencil/paper

Procedures:

Conduct a class discussion around the following questions:

Have you ever worked very hard at something you felt was not understood or appreciated? What was it? What was said or done that made you feel your effort was not appreciated?

Have you ever wanted to share things — ideas, feelings, something you've written or made — but were afraid to? Were you afraid that people might put you or it down? What kinds of things might they say or do that would put you, your ideas, or your achievement down?

Introduce the concept of "killer statements and gestures" to the students. All of us have many feelings, thoughts, and creative behaviors that are killed off by other people's negative comments, physical gestures, etc. Some killer statements that are often used (even by teachers!) are:

We don't have time for that now.
That's a stupid idea. You know that's impossible.
You're really weird!
Are you crazy? kidding me? serious?
Only girls/boys do that!
Wow, he's strange, man, really strange!
That stuff is for sissies.

Tell the students that they're going to be social science researchers for the next 24 hours. Ask them to keep a record of all the killer statements they hear in school, at lunch, at home, and at play. Discuss the findings with them the next time the group meets.

To wrap-up ask each student to make a list of five positive statements that he might give to a friend/family member/teacher. This positive statement should tell something that the student appreciates about the person.

Belonging

Objectives:
To discuss the feelings of being "included/excluded."
To plan specific actions to include others in activities.

Time:
One session

Materials:
Green, blue, and yellow dots, pencil, paper
(if group is large another color or two may be added)

Procedures:

The teacher gives a brief explanation of non-verbal behavior then explains to the students that a colored dot is going to be placed on the forehead of each person. The colored dot represents a group that they are going to join.

The rules of the game are:

1. No talking!
2. Students must use only non-verbal behavior to discover the color of their dot and to form a group with those who have dots of the same color.

The teacher begins the "no talking" time and goes around and places the dots on the forehead of each student (without them seeing the color). The teacher selects one student (preferably one who is popular and accepted by others) to get the yellow dot. Then he/she instructs the students to form a group (using non-verbal behavior) with those who have the same color dot.

It will soon become apparent that this one student is not a part of any group. Ask the student to relate his/her feelings about being left out. Then involve the other students in a discussion on "How it feels to be excluded." "What can we do to include others?" "Do new students feel this way?" Discuss the nonverbal behavior that students used to let others know that they were included or excluded.

In closing ask each student to make a special effort during the week to make another person feel included.

F

What If ...

Objective:
To identify times when we were able to control ourselves.

Time:
One session

Procedures:
Organize the students into small groups of 3 or 4.
Give each group one of the "What If" situations below.

What if ...
1. your family found your porch steps painted orange?
2. the windows of your home were splattered with broken eggs?
3. the hedge bordering your yard was broken and your mother's flowers were trampled?
4. someone put a dead rat in your mailbox?
5. the sidewalk in front of your house had insults and dirty words written on it?
6. someone broke a window in your house and then ran away?
7. you found your father's car tires slashed?

Ask each group to discuss reactions to these questions by using some of the following (you may want to make a copy of these questions for each group):

1. How do you think you would feel if you were involved in any of the above situations?
2. How do you suppose you would act in such situations?
3. What feelings would people be trying to satisfy by destroying things like that?
4. What needs might such a person have?
5. How might a person who vandalizes feel about something that belonged to someone else?
6. How do you think that person may feel about himself?
7. When you are very angry with someone, how do you behave?
8. How would destroying someone's property be different from physically hurting that person?
9. How would you feel after you had destroyed something of someone else's?
10. Are there positive ways of "blowing off steam?"

Share feelings with group as a whole; include members' experiences.

Related activity:

Introduce the following topic: "A time I wanted to blow up but didn't."
As students share their stories about almost blowing up at brothers, teachers, parents, and others, encourage them to describe how it feels to control one's temper. Ask them whether they think little kids can control their tempers as well as older kids. Ask them why they think as they do. Encourage them to discuss what they do when they feel like blowing up. (I used to throw rocks at bottles that I had lined up on the railroad tracks or smash orange crates with a hammer.)

Feelings Display

Objectives:
To be able to identify feelings students have experienced.
To be able to discuss how these feelings effect students' lives.

Time:
One session

Materials:
Worksheet: "Feelings Display"

Procedures:

Hand out the worksheet and have students complete the work, following the directions at the top.

When students have completed the worksheet, carry on a class discussion using such questions as those listed below:

What does it feel like to be ...?

What causes us to have certain feelings?

Which feelings are "good?" Which are "bad?"

Which feelings do you experience most often?

How can you deal with negative feelings?

Feelings Display

Work alone at first. Then sit with others and share your ideas.

1. **Put a plus sign by each of the feelings that you experienced in the last week.**

2. **Put an X by the feelings that you rarely or never experience.**

3. **Write in some additional feelings that you sometimes have.**

curious	contented or fulfilled	excited	warm and cozy	safe and secure
humble	strong and capable		hopeful	loveable
optimistic	silly		bored	envious of others
	childish	hurt	rebellious	
nervous	jealous		empty	irritated
	worried	disgusted	guilty	
mean and destructive	terrified	scared or afraid	furious	depressed

"I Feel Good About..."

Objectives:

To provide an opportunity for students to share feelings with others and to be able to appreciate differences among people

Time:

One session

Materials:

Large sheet of white paper, colored markers, ink pad

Procedures:

Tape a very large sheet of plain white paper on the wall or board. Have plenty of colored markers ready and one ink pad. Tell the students that you are going to talk about differences. Let them name ways we are all different. Many will suggest the obvious (eyes, names, families, etc.). Explain that our fingerprints are also a unique and identifying physical feature. Each of our thumbprints is a special mark unlike no other! add that our feelings on the inside are also different from others.

Now, you set the pattern to follow. Stamp your own thumbprint on the paper. Then write, *I feel good about* _____ and fill in the blank according to your feelings. Write your words around your fingerprint.

Kids will be eager to try. Let them, one at a time until everyone has his/her mark and feelings on the paper.

Wrap-up:

Read over and admire the final work. Help students notice their uniqueness as well as the uniqueness of others.

G

Friends — Lost and Found

Objective:
To help students will recognize the changing aspect of friendships.

Time:
One session

Procedures:

1. Adviser initiates discussion about how friendships develop. Use the "Teacher Reference" list for starters.
2. Put the Student Questions on the board or hand out separately to each group of four or five.
3. If there is time or interest, the entire group could share some of their answers.

TEACHER REFERENCE FOR DISCUSSION

The following are some reasons for choosing friends?

1. Common likes and dislikes.
2. Personality traits (i.e., humor)
3. Physical appearance.
4. Social status.
5. Peer pressure.
6. Family background.
7. Needs fulfillment.

STUDENT QUESTIONS

1. What is a friend?

2. What kind of people are not your friends?

3. What makes and breaks friendships?

4. What makes friendships change?

5. Write a list of what you want in a friend

Duck's Best Friends

Objective:
To learn to evaluate the effects and consequences of behavioral choice

Time:
One session

Materials:
"Duck's Best Friends" handout

Procedures:

Distribute "Duck's Best Friends" to each student. (Allow oral or silent reading, depending upon the class reading level.)

Following reading of the story say to the group:

  Scientists have studied friends and friendships by surveying many, many people. Here are some things they have learned:

a. Most people don't suddenly decide to be friends. Friendships grow.
b. Being able to share ideas and feelings is important between friends.
c. Friends trust each other. People say friends are loyal and don't talk about each other in a bad way.
d. Friends feel good being together and so often seek each other out.
e. Real friends don't care what you wear, or whether you are good at soccer, etc.; they care about the kind of person you are.
f. Separation doesn't end a friendship — people can be apart for years and when reunited, still be friends.
g. People who have good friends are usually happier and healthier than people who do not have friends.
h. The younger you are the more likely you are to be influenced by a friend.

Ask the students to discuss the following questions:

a. Why is it hard for a single member of a group to go against the actions of the group?
b. What is peer pressure?
c. How can a person do what he or she believes is right and still have friends?
d. Is it necessary to conform to be liked or popular?
e. If a group you are with is doing something that you want no part of, how should you handle it?

DUCK'S BEST FRIENDS
by
Ann-Marie Drozd

BANG! The classroom door hit hard against the wall. Books flew into the room and dropped to the floor.

Then a teenager followed the books into the room. He fell to the floor, too, — with a thud! The seated students laughed. From the back of the room a voice called, "It's Dan the Duck!"

"Yeah," added another voice, "Old duck-foot Dan has done it again!"

The face of the young man on the floor turned red. But he smiled and picked himself up. He knew the other kids liked to tease and joke around him. But he didn't mind. They are my friends, he told himself.

At the end of the class the teenagers moved out into the hall. As one group walked along, they heard a voice behind them.

"Hey, gang. Wait up!"

"Oh, no," Jerry said. "Here comes Duck again. Let's get out of here."

"No, wait," said Ray. "Let's have some fun with him."

The group watched as Dan walked ducklike down the hall toward them.

"Hi, gang," Dan said after catching up. "Thanks for waiting."

"Think nothing of it, Duck. We loved watching you *fall in* today," said Ray. "Great show. You're getting better and better."

Dan's face turned red. "I know," he said. "I...lost my footing."

"Couldn't happen to a nicer boy," Karen added with a laugh. "Say, have you ever thought of trying out for the swim team? Ducks do great in water."

Dan smiled, "I can't swim."

"A duck that can't swim!" said Karen. That made everyone laugh even louder. But Dan didn't mind the teasing. Friends always tease each other, he thought.

"You don't have to swim to be on the basketball team, Duck," said Ray. "Why not try out for that?"

"Sure, Duck," added Jerry, "we could use you. We need someone to go after runaway balls. My dog used to — but he broke his leg." The group roared with laughter again.

"Do...do you all want to come over to my house?" Dan asked. "I have some great new records and lots of stuff to eat. My brother Jake is picking me up and..."

"Uh...thanks, Duck" said Jerry, looking for a way out. "But Ray and I have ...uh...basketball practice."

"And Karen and I said we would stay and watch," added Carla.

"Well, OK...sure! OK! said Dan. "See you Monday, gang."

After Duck left, Ray turned to Carla. "Don't you have to go right home, Carla?" he asked.

"I do. but so what?" Carla said. "There is no basketball practice either. You were lying, too."

"Maybe you should have gone, Carla," Jerry teased. "You could have gone in the car with Duck and Jake. You know that his brother is good-looking."

"Sure," said Carla. "Duck's brother is all right! But who wants to be seen with a creep like Duck?"

"Besides," said Karen, "Duck would trip you before you got to the car door." The four laughed louder than ever.

Later the four headed for Ray's house. By the time they got there, they had forgotten about Duck. No one ever saw him on weekends.

But when classes began the following Monday, Ray saw that Duck was not in his seat.

"Where's Duck?" Ray asked Jerry. "Isn't it time for his act?"

"Haven't seen him yet," Jerry answered. "But he'll be here. I saw his brother's car parked outside of school."

"Duck will drop in any minute now," said Carla with a laugh.

"Watch the door," said Karen. "The show is about to start."

The classroom door did open. And a young man walked in. His arms were filled with books.

"Wow! It's Jake," Karen said to Carla. "He *is* beautiful!"

For a while Jake and the teacher talked quietly. Then Jake turned to face the waiting class.

"Dan won't be …," Jake began. His voice cracked — then stopped. Everyone could see the tears in his eyes. After a few seconds he began to talk again.

"Dan had this sickness," Jake said. "He didn't want anyone to know — to feel sorry for him. But I know all of you could tell. He had such a hard time walking."

"But Dan always had good friends at this school. You, Carla — and Ray and Jerry and you, Karen. he was always talking about all of you. He said you teased him a lot. But he knew you really liked him."

"So I just wanted to come here and thank you — for…understanding." Then Jake was gone.

The room was quiet for a long time after Jake left. Duck's four friends sat looking at the floor.

Their faces were bright red. Tears ran down their faces. Everyone knew. Everyone knew all about how Karen and Ray and Carla and Jerry had been — DUCK'S BEST FRIENDS.

G

Friendship Checklist

Objective:
To become aware of the expectations people have about friends.

Time:
One session

Materials:
"Friendship Checklist" for each group

Procedures:

Groups consisting of from four to six pupils may be formed after they have individually marked the checklist. With a student serving as group leader a short discussion is held to determine the correctness of the statement. In the event of disagreement, a vote is taken and the majority vote will rule. After discussion, pupils will count their correct answers to determine their score. This activity is also suited for large group discussion with the teacher serving as group leader.

Wrap-up:

a. Was anyone voted down on the correct answer to the statements?
When you were voted down, did you change your mind about the correct answer? Is it easy to change your mind or attitude about these things?
b. Which of the above statements suggest qualities that you wish your friends had?
c. Which of the above are true of you?

Friendship Checklist

1. _____   A friend is a person who makes you feel good.

2. _____   New friends are the best.

3. _____   Friends understand you better than others.

4. _____   True friendships seldom last very long.

5. _____   Friends never hurt you.

6. _____   A friend is someone who your parents like.

7. _____   Good friends stick up for you when you are wrong.

8. _____   Friends should share secrets.

9. _____   To have friends, you need to have money to spend on them.

10. _____   To keep friends, you must be honest with them.

G

Friends Are ...

Objective:
To help students develop an increased awareness of the concepts related to friendships.

Time:
One session

Materials:
"Friends Are..." handout, posterboard, markers

Procedures:

Have students discuss friendship for several minutes, what friendship is to them.

Suggested Topics:
   a. How do you choose your friends?
   b. What are some qualities of a good friend?
   c. Do you have the characteristics of a good friend?
   d. Do people judge you by your friends?
   e. In what ways are my friends like me?
   f. Why do you need friends?
   g. What kinds of pressures do my friends put on me?
   h. Do I have the qualities I value in a friend?

After some discussion distribute handout for the students to complete.

When finished with the handout, have the students get in groups of three to five. Pass out the posterboard and have each group list five reasons for having friends. Have the students decide on a title for their poster. Put them up in the room to remind students that friends really are a "necessary" part of their lives.

Related activity:
1. Ask your students, "What qualities do you look for in a friend? What qualities are important to a friendship?
2. Use the chalkboard to make a list of these qualities. Be sure to include every quality the students suggest for the list.
3. After students have brainstormed, ask them to copy the list on paper.
4. Now request students to ask themselves, "Which qualities of friendship do *I* have? Have the students place a
   ✓   in front of the qualities you possess
   ✓+   in front of your strongest qualities
   ✓-   in front of the qualities in which you need to improve.

This activity helps students develop awareness of themselves as friends.

Friends Are?

1. Friends are

2. My best friend is

3. Friendship is

4. I was friendly to someone when

5. We need friends because

6. Having a friend is

7. I trust friends because

8. I can tell secrets to my friends because

9. To be a friend is

10. When I talk to my friend I

G

Peer Relations/A Friend Is...

Objective:
To help students identify admired characteristics in friends and compare them with their own characteristics.

Time:
One or two sessions

Materials:
"A Friend is ...," handout

Procedures:

1. Distribute worksheet "A Friend is..."

2. Have students fill in the ten lines (Column 1) with the ten characteristics they most prize in a friend.

3. Let students complete Column 2 on their own.

4. Discuss the following questions:

   a. Can you see yourself as a friend?
   b. Are there characteristics that you would like to have?
   c. What are some ways you could get these? (be with people who have the admired characteristics, think about your actions toward others)

A Friend Is ...

COLUMN 1	COLUMN 2

A friend is ... does ...	This describes me		
	Usually	Sometimes	Seldom
1.			
2.			
3.			
4.			
5.			
6.			
7			
8.			

G

Friendship Poems

Objective:
To identify qualities of a friend

Time:
One or two sessions

Materials:
Markers, pieces of construction
paper 3" x 4" (approx)

Procedures:

1. Discuss some of the characteristics of friendship.

2. Ask the students to complete the statement: "Friendship is ..."

3. Students should write their ending on a piece of scrap paper.

4. After the students have their ending finalized, have them write just the ending
   on a sentence strip.

5. Display groups of the sentences on a wall or bulletin board in poetry form.

6. Examples:

   Friendship is ...
          feeling love,
          going to a movie together,
          watching a sunset with someone,
          knowing you don't have to say anything

The In-Crowd

Objective:

To identify how peer pressure can effect membership in a group

Time:

One session

Materials:

"In-Crowd" handout for each student

Procedures:

Brief discussion of need people have to belong to a group, (Moose, Kiwanis, Girl Scouts, etc.) and the rules some have about membership (male only, certain religions, etc.)

"Just how far will people go to feel a part of something?"

Distribute handout.

Later, you may want students to get into small groups to share their answers or share aloud as a group.

THE IN-CROWD

Frannie wants to join a certain crowd of kids at school, but the group has a test of courage for members: you have to steal $50.00 worth of stuff from a discount store before the group will accept you.

Fran walks out of school, confused about what to do. She would die if she were caught stealing. But more than anything, Fran wants to be in with that one group. "I'm always on the outside," she says to herself as she crosses the street. "If I could get in with those kids, I would really have fun for a change."

Work alone at first. Then sit with others and share your ideas.

1. If there were 100 people like Frannie, how many of them do you think would try to steal the merchandise and pass the group's test?

2. What do you think of the group's test for membership?

3. Do you know of groups that have rules or expectations for new members? What are the requirements?

4. Have you ever been in a situation that was anything like Frannie's?

   What happened?

   How did you feel?

EXTRA

5. If you have time, try writing a story or drawing a picture showing what Frannie might do, and perhaps how she felt, and how things worked out in the end. You might even try writing two different stories with two different endings.

Doubting Debbie

Objective:
To identify problems associated with peer pressure.

Time:
One session

Materials:
Worksheets

Procedures:

Say to students:

> There are times when we find ourselves in troublesome situations. We really don't know what to do. It may be that we did something that caused a problem, or it may be that something just turned out that way.
>
> When we don't know which way to turn, when things seem to be more than we can deal with, it helps to stop and think things through. Today you will have a chance to think things through and identify some problems.

Hand out worksheets and read the example re: "Debbie" aloud to students.

After they have had time to complete the worksheet call for a show of hands on the questions on the bottom of the handout.

Encourage individual responses from volunteers.

? DOUBTING DEBBIE

Debbie would really like to have Marsha as a friend. Marsha has invited Debbie and several other girls to a party at her house. Debbie knows that some of the girls invited will smoke cigarettes and that she would be expected to smoke if she went to the party. Debbie has never smoked and she doesn't wish to start. She has some doubts about going to the party.

If Debbie goes to the party, or if she decides not to go to the party, there could be some problems.

What problems could come up if she decided to go?

Example: They would laugh at her if she didn't smoke.

What problems could come up if she decided *not* to go?

Go back and check over your list of problems. Should Debbie go to the party? Depending on your answer, which problem will provide the greatest challenge for Debbie?

Peer Pressure Situations

Objective:

To help students consider options available to them in different situations

Time:
One or two sessions

Materials:
"Peer Pressure Situations" handout

Procedures:

Use the situations on the handout for role playing exercises.

Discussion may follow each role-play regarding other alternatives, effectiveness of solutions, etc.

Peer Pressure Situations

1. There is a handicapped girl in your school and many of the kids tease her in the halls. Your best friend thinks it's awful to tease her, but when "everyone" is around she does too. Try to influence her to change her opinion.

2. Sue and you are best friends, but lately Sue has been rebellious and distant from you. You hear she's on drugs and in with that "burn-out" crowd. How can you try to get her off drugs? (Positive Peer Pressure)

3. Athletics is the "big" thing in your school and you hate all forms of it. Everyone is always bugging you to try out, but you don't care to. How do you stand up to them? (Use two kids here to pressure you.)

4. Nobody in school hangs around with their parents, because it isn't "cool." You really enjoy your parents and go out with them often. The kids really give you guff. How do you take this and show them that parents aren't bad?

5. You and Joe have been going out for two years and now are "in love." Sue, your so-called best friend, comes and tells you that Mark, "the" man in school, wants to date you. She tells you Joe will never know. What do you do? (This can go either way – good or bad.)

6. Books and excellent grades are seen as "dumb" in your school. Nobody likes the "bookies" and leaves them out of everything. You are a "bookie." How do you keep your A grades and be with the kids you want to?

7. Your friends, Sue and Karla, are going out of town to a movie and want you to go with them. Your parents are gone and you're supposed to be baby-sitting your younger sister, but you want to go. What do you do?

8. Your parents are gone and they left you home alone. The kids in school have found out and want you to "host" a party. You know somebody will bring alcohol, but your two friends, John and Dawn, are really pushing you.

9. Expensive clothes are really "in" at school and you can't afford them. You really don't mind not having "neat" clothes, but Sandy and Cindy, the fashionables in your school, really razz you. How do you make them see that clothes really don't matter?

10. You see your best friend, Alice, getting thinner and thinner; in fact she's getting so skinny it's dangerous. Alice thinks she's beautiful and so does her mother. How can you influence them differently and get Alice some help?

Part II

Activities

Second Year

Contents II

NOTE: numbers in parentheses indicate number of related handouts

A

Know Your Neighbors

Objective:

To help students become aware of unique things about their fellow advisory members

Time:
One session

Materials:
"Know Your Neighbor" worksheet
one for each member of the advisory

Procedures:

This activity will help students get acquainted with one another. They are to find someone to sign after each characteristic. The same person should not be used twice. If time permits, the first one who has signatures for all characteristics can identify the persons for the group. The sheets should be retained as some follow-up activities are possible.

Know Your Neighbor

Find someone in class to sign each blank. Do not use the same person more than twice.

1. Has a birthday in the same month as yours _____

2. Is left-handed _____

3. Has the same color outfit as yours _____

4. A person you've never met _____

5. Has three of the same numbers in their phone number _____

6. Someone who likes to ski (water or snow) _____

7. The first letter of their last name is the same as yours _____

8. Has the same number of people in his or her family _____

9. Likes exactly the same favorite TV show _____

10. Loves the same favorite food _____

11. Someone who wears the same shoe size _____

12. Has seen the same movie that you saw last _____

13. Someone who likes spinach _____

14. Someone who has the same color of eyes as yours _____

15. Someone who went to a different school than you did last year _____

16. Someone who has the same PE class _____

17. Someone who plays a musical instrument _____

18. Someone who has lived in a state other than yours _____

A

You Be The Judge

Objective:
To help students know and appreciate appropriate school behaviors and relate them to specific school rules

Time:
Two sessions

Materials:
Worksheet - Role-Playing Situations
School Handbook

Procedures:

Introduce activity by defining *deliberate* and *accidental* and review with class the concepts of behavior and consequences.

Hand out *School Handbook*

Discuss:
- *What are some school rules that everyone knows (expectations)?*
- *What are some school rules you didn't know about?*
- *Can you think of examples of deliberate rule violations?*
- *Can you think of some examples of accidental rule violations?*

Introduce role-playing activity: "You Be The Judge!"

Ask for volunteers to act out the situations. Two students needed for each incident.

After each situation has been acted out, ask:
- *What are the acting and thinking behaviors?*
- *What rules are being broken?*
- *What are the short-term and long-term consequences?*
- *How can the consequences be changed? How can the behaviors be changed?*

Discuss:

- *What school rules are easiest for you to follow? Hardest?*
- *How can you prevent <u>accidental</u> violation of rules (study, know them)*
- *How can you prevent or avoid deliberate violation of rules? (stay away from those who you know violate rules, practice saying "no," etc.)*

Role Playing Situations

(to be cut apart and given to student volunteers)

Ted walks into the math class. He knocks his friend's book onto the floor. Ted is just kidding, but Dave looks angry.

It's lunch time and Nick is walking toward the table. Sam comes up behind him and pushes him. Nick almost falls and swings at Sam. They start fighting.

Karen and Susie are teasing each other about their boy friends while on the school bus. Karen is insulted by something that Susie says. Karen uses profanity as a result of her anger. Susie uses an obscene gesture in response. A loud, profane argument follows. The driver reports the girls' behavior to the principal.

A

Feedback: Human Differences

Objective:

To make students more aware of the individual's likes and dislikes

Time:

One session

Materials:

Copies of "If I Could Be..." sheet
3x5 cards (optional)

Procedures:

There are two options for using this sheet. Choose the one that best fits your group. In both cases, the important factor is the "because" statement.

1. Students can write their statement and answers on a 3x5 card and pin them on themselves. Share these with the entire group. See how many people have the same choices as you.

2. Students could complete feedback sheets individually and then compare them in an open discussion.

If I Could Be...

1. If I could be any animal, I'd be a   because ...

2. If I could be a bird, I'd be a   because ...

3. If I could be an insect, I'd be a   because ...

4. If I could be a tree, I'd be a   because ...

5. If I could be a piece of furniture, I'd be a   because ...

6. If I could be a musical instrument, I'd be a   because ...

7. If I could be a building, I'd be a   because ...

8. If I could be a car, I'd be a   because ...

9. If I could be a state, I'd be   because ...

10. If I could be a game, I'd be   because ...

11. If I could be a record, I'd be   because ...

12. If I could be a TV show, I'd be   because ...

13. If I could be a movie, I'd be   because ...

14. If I could be a food, I'd be   because ...

15. If I could be any color, I'd be   because ...

16. If I could be another person, I'd be   because ...

17. If I could be a teacher I've had, I'd be   because ...

Find the Stone

Objective:

To provide an opportunity for students to become comfortable with one another and informally get acquainted.

Time:

One session

Materials:

3 or 4 small stones, marbles
or small objects

Procedures:

The class sits or stands in a circle and one or more persons are selected to be "finders." The finders go to the center of the circle and close their eyes while the teacher distributes three or four small objects to members of the circle. The members of the circle then pass or pretend to pass the stones around the circle while the finders try to guess who actually has the stones. If the finder guesses correctly, the one caught replaces the finder in the center of the circle.

A

Getting To Know You

Objective:
To assist students in gaining an understanding of how people perceive themselves

Time:
Three sessions

Materials:
Magazines, newspapers, paste, tagboard, scissors

Procedures:

1. On the first day have the students form groups of approximately five people.
2. Each group is assigned a particular category (i.e., automobiles, flowers, animals, restaurants). They are to cut out of the used magazines and newspapers five pictures in their category. Stress to the students to cut out a variety of pictures within their category. For example, if a group is looking for pictures of automobiles, there shouldn't be five pictures of sports cars. Instead their collection should also include station wagons, compact cars, luxury cars, etc.
3. After the groups have cut out their pictures, they mount each one on a separate piece of tagboard.
4. Collect the pictures from the groups after they have mounted them.
5. During the second day, hand back the mounted pictures to the different groups. Ask any one group to divide itself around different areas of the classroom. Each person then holds up his/her mounted picture.
6. The remainder of the class then locates themselves "around" the picture with which they can most closely identify.
7. When students have categorized themselves, ask the people in each category to explain to the person holding the picturetheir rationale for choosing that particular picture. He/she should then make a list of each person's responses.
8. Repeat steps 5-7 with the other categories.
9. The third day, have all students bring to class their list of responses that others made to them on the second day. Lead a discussion about the fact that many times people categorize themselves for different reasons than those in the same category.

Evaluation

Measure the depth of the student's understanding of how people perceive themselves by asking each of them to submit an "I learned" statement on what they learned about themselves and another one on what they learned about others.

Four Corners

Objective:

To demonstrate diversity of opinion while building group cohesiveness

Time:

One session

Materials:

Four signs to be placed or helf up in corners of the room labelled:
> *Strongly agree*
> *Strongly disagree*
> *Tend to disagree*
> *Tend to agree*

Procedures:

This activity works best with a relatively large group, a regular class size.

Make a statement such as the following: *A woman should be President of the United States.*

Give the students a moment to think about the options mentioned above. Then, on signal, ask the students to go to the corner that coincides with their opinion. Allow the students in each corner to discuss briefly among themselves their reasons for choosing that particular corner.

Have one student express to the others why that group chose a certain corner. Be careful to accept each statement and permit some interchange among the group. Permit anyone to change location at this point.

Reassemble the class. Read the statement again and ask the students to go to the corner they feel their parents or teachers would choose. Again, allow time for discussion among those students who selected a particular corner.

Other statements that might be used are the following:

1. Everyone should attend college.
2. Girls can be truck drivers.
3. Students should have the right to choose their own dress code at home, at school, or at work.
4. Giving grades encourages meaningful learning.
5. Parents have a right to plan their children's future.

This activity is readily adaptable for use with current social issues and can be used on many occasions.

— additional topics - continued ➡

A

Four Corners: Additional Topics

What do you think about it?

1. It is good to forget about problems.

2. You should never be embarrassed.

3. Thoughtful people are smart.

4. Boys are better athletes than girls.

5. It is all right for adults to act like children.

6. Everyone becomes bored.

7. People should feel proud.

8. A funny person is well liked.

9. Teachers have a right to feel misunderstood.

10. It is good to get excited.

11. People learn best when they become frustrated.

12. Being happy is not always desirable.

At the close of this activity it is often beneficial to ask each pupil to respond to the questions: "What did you learn?" and "Why is it important to consider another person's point of view?"

Follow-up and/or correlation:

Some of these statements would also serve as starters for circle discussions.

Goal Setting

Objective:
To begin a goal setting process

Time:
Two to four sessions

Background information:

Kick off the year with a series of goal-setting lessons with your students. Goal-setting is a great motivator to all ages as it gives a person a clear direction, purpose and drive. Learning to set goals and seeing them actualized builds individuals' self-esteem, gives them a sense of independence and provides personal satisfaction.

How do you go about teaching this valuable concept? Goal-setting is a step-by-step process that needs to be taught, modeled, and carefully monitored by the teacher or advisor in a series of lessons.

Procedures:

The goal-setting game strategy can be likened to a game of football. The students are team players. The coach (advisor) should review the following information with the class:

HIKE	Select one goal! Make sure the goal is reasonable, specific, and attainable in the near future.
LONG PASS	<u>Think it and ink it!</u> Write the goal as a specific positive statement. Example: *I will spell the days of the week correctly.*
DEFENSE	Then write down the action plan. List all the things that can be done to accomplish the goal.
FUMBLE	Watch out for interferences! Consider all the obstacles that could prevent one from attaining the goal. Example: *There are too many activities in my schedule to allow study time.*

B

TEAM   Name the support team. Write down the names of people who can help you reach your goal and list specific ways each person can help. Tell the goal only to the people who can help you achieve it.

PENALTY   In the goal-setting game saying words like, "I can't, I'll never make it," etc., are penalties that set you back and prevent you from reaching your goal. Replace penalty words with positive cheers like "I know I can."

RELAY   Draw a picture or write a story about yourself achieving the goal. Be sure the paper includes words that describe how good you feel now that the goal has been achieved.

TOUCHDOWN   Put a rock in your pocket to remind you of the goal and every time you touch the rock think about the picture of yourself winning.

Unlike the game of football, goal-setting is a game you cannot lose. Teach the fundamentals of this game to your students and the final score will be a real victory.

GOAL SETTING WORKSHEET

1.   Express your goal in words. Be specific rather than general.

2.   When do you plan to have reached this goal?

3.   Why did you choose this goal? (What will be gained from having reached it?)

4.   Some goals are intangible (like being a happier person). Therefore, they are harder to measure. Tangible goals are easier to measure since they often can be expressed in dollars, hours, people, etc. How are you going to be measuring the progress toward your goal?

5.   What are some problems you may encounter as you work towards your goal?

6.   What is the first step you can take towards your goal?

     When are you going to take this step?

7.   What is the second major step?

     When do you plan to have it completed?

8.   List the other steps and anticipated completion dates for each.

IMPORTANT: NEVER GIVE UP

Self Concept

Objective:

To help students understand the meaning of "Self Concept" and to learn how to build a positive one.

Time:
One or two session

Materials:
Teacher copy of accompanying page

Procedures:

• Write the following four discussion questions on the board and/or read to the class

  1. What does the term "self concept" mean?
  2. What are some ways in which we can help each other's self concept?
  3. What kinds of criticism are the hardest to accept? Why?
  4. What can be learned from accepting criticism thoughtfully?

• Read to the class "Will the Real Bobby Please Stand Up?" and initiate discussion following the reading.

• Read to class "Building a Positive Self Concept." Discuss.

C

Will The Real Bobby Please Stand Up?

Bobby worries a lot about how other people "see" him. At times he even has trouble figuring out who he is and how he should act. He's really good at making people laugh, and he knows his friends enjoy his crazy stunts. But some of his classmates think he's a show-off. Bobby gets uneasy around grownups, too. He likes his parents, although sometimes he's embarrassed when they fuss over him. Bobby likes his teacher, too, but it bothers him when he's told he's immature and fools around too much for his own good.

Like Bobby, we all sometimes feel a little confused about who we are. We are all affected by what other people think of us.

Building A Positive Self Concept

What can you do to develop the positive side of your self-concept? Here are a few guidelines to help you accept the person you are and become the person you want to be:

- Remember, no one is perfect. You have talents and abilities, but you have limitations, too.

- Focus on your strengths and learn to do one thing well. Knowing you can succeed at one activity will give you confidence for trying in other areas as well.

- Set goals for yourself, but be sure they are realistic and limited in number. Give yourself the chance to succeed.

- Try congratulating yourself for your successes instead of blaming yourself for failures.

- Don't moan over your mistakes. Learn from them.

C

Am I Someone Who ...?

Objective:
To help students consider what they value and what they want out of life.

Time:
Two sessions

Materials:
Paper and pencil
Worksheets: "Am I Someone Who?"

Procedures:

Remind students that these questions have no right/wrong answers. They are simply a way for one to reflect on one's values and to see that everyone is not alike in the things he/she values.

1. Pass out worksheets to students and give them time to complete the sheet individually with a *yes, no,* or brief comment .

2. Then have students compare their responses with a partner.

(A possible variation for later in the year would be to have each student in the pair tell how he/she *think* his/her partner would have responded.

3. To bring closure the following questions can be used.

   Is it okay to be different?

   How did you feel about having different feelings from others?

   How did you feel when others made statements about you?

Am I Someone Who ...?

1. Needs to be alone?

2. Watches television soap operas?

3. Judges someone by first appearances?

4. Is afraid to be alone in the dark?

5.. Is afraid of trying new experiences?

6. Is capable of handling different situations on my own?

7. Experiences boredom and lacks motivation?

8. Likes to take over leadership responsibilities?

9. Is easily swayed by the latest fads?

10. Tries to do everything as perfectly as possible?

11. Likes to work with other people more than alone?

12. Considers loyalty to a friend or cause more important than honesty?

13. Would rather fight than quit?

14. Would donate my body to medical research?

15. Has a close friend of another race?

16. Has been hurt by a friend?

17. Would like to make some changes in my life?

18. Would rather be someone else?

19. Thinks it's all right for older brothers and sisters to discipline younger ones?

20. Would rather be older or younger than I am now?

C

Star Traits

Objective:
To identify goals for our own self-improvement by recognizing what we admire in others.

Time:
One session

Materials:
Handout: "Star Traits"

Procedures:

Inform students that they should take their time in listing five people they admire. They can consider fictional characters from books, historical figures from the past or present, or people they know.

The personality traits they associate with the five people are to be listed, then ranked according to importance. Let each student determine what traits are the most important or the least important.

After sharing their lists, encourage students to make CONNECTIONS with the listed traits and the traits they would consider most important for a politician to have, a physician to have, and an attorney to have. Do this by saying: "On your list of traits, which trait would be most important for a politician to have? a banker to have? etc...."

All life forms have traits to be admired. It's a matter of finding them.

☆ STAR TRAITS

1.

2.

3.

4.

5.

Which five people, past or present, real or fictional, do you admire the **MOST?**

Suppose you could mold their qualities together to form a very SPECIAL PERSON!

DO IT BY LISTING THEIR SPECIAL TRAITS HERE:

RANK

1 →

2 →

3 →

4 →

5 →

6 →

7 →

8 →

9 →

10 →

Now rank the traits by their importance, 1 (highest) thru 10 (lowest)

My best trait is

Something else about me is

C

Myself, and Me Alone

Objective:
To help students to become aware of their uniqueness

Time:
One session

Materials:
Construction paper, tag board,
poster board, crayon, colored pencils or pens

Procedures:

Put on board or overhead:
An "acrostic" spells out a word or words in one direction while comments on the word or words are made in another direction. here is an acrostic written by a teacher in a student's autograph book:

> B-eautiful
> E-nthusiastic
> T-ruthful
> S-ensitive to feelings of others
> Y-es, you are all of these things!

A.   Ask students to make an acrostic using the letters of their name, describing themselves as they really are.

B.   Then ask them to do another one describing themselves as they'd like to be.

C.   If time permits and products seem to justify it, suggest that they illustrate the acrostics on a board with pens, crayons, etc. Display on the bulletin board.

C

Sharing Likes and Dislikes

Objective:

To make students aware of ways in which people are alike and different

Time: **Materials:**

One session   Paper and pencil

Procedures:

Read the following list to students and have each of them write something he/she either likes or dislikes after each numbered item.

1.	Food	7.	Movie
2.	TV show	8.	Indoor game
3.	Summer vacation	9.	Outdoor game
4.	Saturday night	10.	Chore at home
5.	Class	11.	Money
6.	Gift received	12.	Hobby

After students have responded individually, they move around to find someone who shares the same like or dislike and write the name of that student by it. One point is given for each match. High point person wins.

The teacher should stress the sharing of similarities. Encourage the awareness and acceptance of personal values held by others.

Bug List

Objectives:

To assist pupils in identifying behaviors that they find bothersome. To provide a way for pupils to discover how different behaviors are received by different people

Time:
Two sessions

Materials:
Butcher paper, paints, markers, paper/pencils

Procedures:

To introduce this activity discuss "bugging behavior." To get the students talking the following questions may help:

1. What does it mean when people say that they are being bugged?
2. Is it fun to be bugged?
3. How do you feel when someone is bugging you?
4. Do you feel friendly to people that bug you?

Close the discussion at an appropriate time and ask pupils to make a list of the "five things" that bug them the most. After the list is completed, have pupils rank their "bothersome bugs" from one to five, the most bothersome being number one.

Next, have pupils list their Number One Bug on the chalkboard and sign their name so that it may be identified. Discussion may follow in order to identify the things that students find bothersome. Attention should be called to the variety of behaviors listed, the contrasting behaviors, and the likeness of bugging behaviors. From the list it may be possible to determine the Number One Bug of the entire group.

Optional activities:

1. Discuss the following topics:
   a. What might you do to let people know that they are bugging you?
   b. What might you do to stop people from bugging you?
   c. Can you think of anything you do or say that might bug others?

2. Engage pupils in making "Don't Bug Me by _____" posters. Pupils may also make "Don't Bug Me" badges on which they would write their **Number One Bug**.

C

Partner Risk

Objectives:

To provide students with an opportunity to share personal feelings with a partner
To develop trust among members of the advisory group

Time:

One session

Materials:

Discussion topics of interest to students
in the group, one on each of 10 file cards.

Procedures:

Place each of the following topics on a card. (You can, of course, substitute others.)

A time my brother (sister) got me in trouble
A time I acted cool to impress someone
A time I wanted to leave school
A time I was afraid I would get caught
A time I didn't know whether or not to tell.
A time someone pretended to be my friend but wasn't
A time I misbehaved to get attention
A time I wished I was an only child
A time someone got me in trouble
A time I like to remember

Students working in pairs are given a topic to discuss for a few minutes. If time permits a second topic may be given to each pair, or pairs can be reconstituted with different persons..

Following one or more discussion periods, the teacher asks the students to close their eyes and think about the following questions:

(1) Were you really listened to? Did your partner really hear you? Did you listen to him/her?

(2) Did you really share your feelings or did you screen them before talking about them?

(3) Did you worry that you talked too much? Too little?

(4) Would you have added to your discussion if you had had more time?

(continued on next page)

C

(5) Were you mostly a "pickee" (one who was chosen by another when partners were switched), or a "picker" (one who did the choosing)? Suggestion: Next time reverse roles. If you were a "picker," try to be a "pickee." Which would you rather be?

(6) Was your partner like you or quite different from you? Can you understand him? Do you like having a partner who is like you? Different from you?

(7) Would you like your partner to have some of your experiences? Would you like to have some of his/hers?

Additional or alternate topics that could be used for discussion

(1) Tell a point in the work experience of one of your parents that was a turning point in your life.

(2) Tell of an experience you had related to a department or grocery store.

(3) Describe how your life would change if there were no T.V.

(4) Talk about your allowance — how much you get, when and how, whether you think it's fair, and how you usually spend it.

(5) Tell about a movie which touched you deeply.

(6) Talk about one or more things you would like to be able to do better socially, intellectually or athletically (or as a family member, citizen, or friend, etc.)

Consider the Issues

Objective:
To help students consider one another's opinions on issues related to self-esteem

Time:
One or two sessions

Materials:
Student handout of discussion questions and quotes on self-esteem

Procedures:

Discuss the questions in small groups or use the inner/outer circle technique. This technique works as follows:

1. Have students in the inner circle begin the discussion. Let them talk together for 6 to 8 minutes, then call time.

2. Have the observers in the outer circle report on what they saw and heard while the inner group listens in silence. Then let the inner group comment on the observer's reports and the discussion itself.

3. Have the groups reverse roles and repeat the above.

4. Evaluate the discussion by asking students what helped or hurt it.

Variation: You can leave one chair empty in the inner circle so a member of the outer circle may enter, contribute and then leave.

5. The "Quotes on Self-esteem" may be used to elicit further thinking and discussion. Teacher could read them one at a time discussing each after reading or copies of all could be given to students.

DISCUSSION QUESTIONS RELATED TO SELF-ESTEEM

1. What is the difference between bragging and saying positive things about yourself?

2. Do you think the development of good self-esteem is more difficult for boys or girls? Explain the reasons for your answer.

3. How could annoying characteristics that a person might have, like being a bully, a loud-mouth, conceited, or critical be a reflection of low self-esteem?

4. Give examples of how low self-esteem may cause problems for an individual when:

   a. talking with new people

   b. admitting she/he is wrong

   c. accepting constructive criticism

   d. expressing ideas that differ from other people's

5. How would you advise parents to help their children build strong self-esteem?

6. How can you help others raise their self-esteem?

7. Are most people too easy to too hard on themselves? Why?

8. What are some things that our school does (or that individual teachers do) to build self-confidence in students?

9. What are some things that our school does that tears down student self-confidence?

QUOTES ON SELF-ESTEEM

A person who doubts himself is like a man who would enlist in the ranks of his enemies and use weapons against himself. He makes his failure certain by himself being the first person to be convinced of it.

— Alexander Dumas

If you are not for you, who will be? If you are only for you, what's the purpose?

— Hillel

Once a young boy was asked by a man what he could do better than anyone else. It was the assumption of the man who asked the question that everyone has some special thing at which he excels. The question was intended to help the boy discover his best quality or talent in order to increase his self-esteem. But the answer that the boy gave surprised the man. For the boy, who seemed very self-assured, replied, "I can be me better than anyone else in the word."

This is the perfect answer to the man's question. Each one of us can be the unique person that we are, better than anyone else. We are all best at being our different and unique selves.

If someone said, "Look, I'm a terrible person and I like it that way; leave me alone," chances are he wouldn't mean it. Most people are quite unhappy about making themselves miserable; there is usually a severe inner struggle going on. Part of the person is pushing himself down, but another part is crying out that that's not where he belongs.

— from *How To Be Your Own Best Friend*

It would seem like a good idea for schools to follow the precept I saw printed on an automobile drag strip racing program: "Every effort is made to ensure that each entry has a reasonable chance of victory."

— William W. Purkey
Self-Concept and School Achievement

If we can't make peace with ourselves as we are, we never will be able to make peace with ourselves. This requires the courage to be imperfect, the realization that I make mistakes, that I have faults ... I don't have to be better than others ... which is a tremendous relief if you accept that.

— Rudolph Dreikurs
The Courage To Be Imperfect

I'm afraid to tell you who I am because I'm the only me I've got and you might not like it.

— Patricia, 13

Finish each day and be done with it. You have done what you could. Some blunders and absurdities no doubt crept in; forget them as soon as you can. Tomorrow is a new day and is too dear with its hopes and invitations to waste a moment on the yesterday..

— Ralph Waldo Emerson

D

One Thing I Like About Myself

Objectives:

To help students learn how difficult it is to share by providing opportunities for them to share statements with others and focus on the positive qualities they all possess

Time:

One session

Procedures:

Leader gives directions and stresses importance of sharing positive rather than negative qualities.

Each person is asked to state one positive thing he/she likes about himself/herself. Model this activity and go around the room as many times as possible.

To bring closure use such questions as these:

Is it easy or difficult to share positive characteristics about oneself? Why?

Are others aware of the positive characteristics you revealed? Why? Why not?

D

Keeping Mistakes From Lowering
Your Self-Esteem

Objective:

Students will handle mistakes in a manner that does not erode self-esteem

Time:

One session

Materials:

Student handout "How To Keep Mistakes
From Lowering Your Self-Esteem"

Procedures:

Have students read through the sets of comments on the handout. Encourage a discussion
to clarify the meaning of each one.

How To Keep Mistakes From Lowering Your Self-esteem

Low self-esteem is like a magnifying glass that can make a small mistake seem like a huge failure. Too many people put themselves down when they make mistakes or fail at something. They need to realize that mistakes and failures don't take away their value as a person. Read through the statements below. Put a star by the ones you think provide the best advice about how to handle a mistake. When we are through put it in your notebook or some place where you can read it again if you find you're being hard on yourself when you make a mistake.

Accept the fact that making mistakes is an important part of learning. When you make a mistake you can make yourself feel better by looking back and noticing how far you have come. You are improving all the time. Notice that, not just your mistakes.

When you fail at something say things to yourself like, "So I made a mistake because I'm human." "Everybody makes mistakes, I'll just try again." "I do okay at some things and fail at other things, just like everybody else," or "I've got the right to be wrong sometimes."

The most important thing to do when you make a mistake is to fix it. Think of learning to do things better.

It takes time to develop certain skills. New actions are bound to be awkward the first time through. This is not a problem unless you think you need everything to be perfect the first time. Accept mistakes as a natural part of living that in no way takes away your value as a person.

Sure, it feels good to succeed but it is not awful to make mistakes. Everybody makes them and people are not any less valuable or lovable when they do. Mistakes are just inconvenient and tell us that things need to be done in a different way.

When you make a mistake the most important thing to remember is to forgive yourself again and again. Treat yourself like a good friend would. Try and be gentle with yourself. Realize that you're a good person even if you slip up now and then.

D

Creative Art Experience

Objectives:
To generate creativity and imagination in individuals while sharing themselves
To acquaint students with art and imagination

Time:
One or two sessions

Materials:
Large sheets of paper, sheets of colored paper, collage materials, catalogues, magazines, post cards, etc., glue, tape, crayons, felt tip pens

Procedures:

1. A day or two before, ask students to bring magazines, etc., to class.
2. Choose one of the following activities:

    "Advertisement for Myself":   Participants are asked to make up a brochure advertising themselves.

    "Self-Collage":   Individuals represent their positive self-image by making a collage.

    Announce it to the group. Discuss possible examples of what could be done.

3. When students are finished, discuss the following:

    How can we display our work?
    What did you learn about yourself from this?
    What else could these advertisements (collages) be used for?

Follow up on the answer to the first question by posting work in the room.

Doodle Art: With very free motions, have the students draw one continuous doodle line (this can be done with one or more colors or patterns of color to finish off their design).

> *Did you ever try some doodle art,*
> *It's so much fun to do.*
> *You make a squiggle or a curve,*
> *And add a line or two.*
> *You turn it this way and that,*
> *And very soon you'll see*
> *A bird, a man, oh anything,*
> *As plain as plain can be.*

(continued on next page)

D

Variations:

1. Have the children doodle to music.

2. Not looking, have students draw objects on paper.

3. Students may want to use a geometric design, filling in spaces with different ideas on the same shapes.

4. Have students cut out one shape, place it about the paper, tracing it each time. Then they can color in the shapes and the overlaps.

Use Imagination!

Children love to imagine!

Communication Overview

Objectives:
To help students become more aware of why communication with others is not always easy
To encourage them to think about ways to improve their own communication skills

Time:
One to three sessions

Materials:
Handout "Communication is Complicated" (3 pages)

Procedures:

1. Distribute handout.

2. Read the introduction aloud as the students follow along.

3. Stop as indicated and ask students to think about the passage and briefly write down answers.

4. Ask students to share what they have written. (Perhaps a personal example from you would help them understand better or encourage them to share their own examples.) The discussion is an important part of helping students realize how communication skills or lack or them affect their everyday lives.

5. Ask students to look at the picture, "What do you see?" Most will see a vase *or* two faces. Point out that there are different ways to look at the same thing, and when people assume everyone sees exactly what they do, problems often arise (e.g., values, conflicts, religious and political differences, generation gap, clothes, and hair styles.).

6. If time permits student volunteers could model examples of nonverbal language that conflict with the verbal message.

Communication is Complicated

Communication is simply receiving and sending messages — understanding and being understood. Everything we do and say is a form of communication, whether it be a hand signal, a shrug of the shoulders, a facial expression, or a verbal message. Communicating with others is something we all take for granted, but poor communication can cause problems for all of us.

There are several reasons why difficulties may arise when we send messages or receive messages from other people. Sometimes the messages we send are confusing to other people. When we say one thing with words yet another with actions, it is easy for others to misinterpret our message. Try to remember an incident when you sent a confusing message — saying one thing with your words and another with your actions. What difficulties did that confusing message cause you or someone else?

QUESTION
What confusing message have you sent?

QUESTION
Why did it cause another person to be confused?

Sometimes we receive a message that we don't understand. It could be because the message to us was unclear; or it could be that we *expected* the sender to say or do one thing, and when the sender said or did something else, we didn't understand. That may have caused us to become confused or even angry because our expectations weren't met.

Example: Your best friend gets on the school bus, walks past you, and never even says "Hi!" He always sits beside you on the bus; you even saved a seat for him!

The message you receive is, "I don't want to sit with you anymore. I've got other people I'd rather sit with."

The fact may be that this morning he had a big fight with his parents and ran out of the house, almost missing the bus. He was still very upset and wasn't willing or ready to talk to anyone. He didn't want to ride the bus or go to school at all.

QUESTION
Can you think of a time when you became angry or your feelings were hurt because you expected one kind of behavior and received another? Briefly describe the situation and how it made you feel.

Another roadblock to good communication involves how we view or perceive a person or situation. People often see the same thing differently and cannot understand why another person does not share their point of view. Have you ever dressed for school in the morning, thinking you looked "pretty cool," only to come downstairs and have your mother or father say, "I refuse to let you go to school looking like that. You look AWFUL! Go upstairs and change this minute."?

QUESTION
Who is right and who is wrong in this kind of a situation? Could it just be that your parents "see" what you are wearing differently than you do?

Have you ever looked at or perceived something differently than someone else? Did it cause problems? Why? Briefly describe the situation and the problem it caused.

Look at the picture below. What do you see? Does everyone in your class see the same thing? Is there one right answer and one wrong answer? What makes you see the picture differently from other people in your class

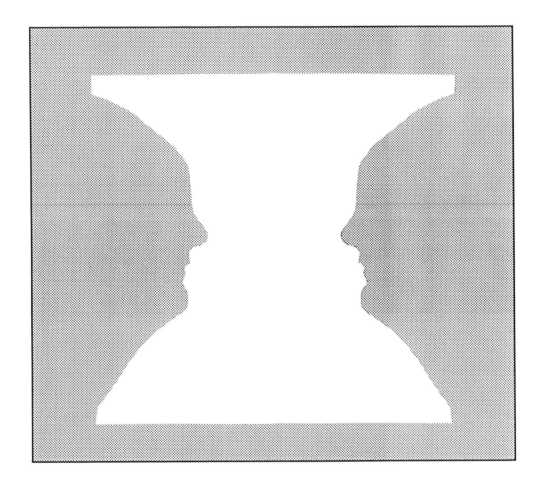

Thus far we have talked about three roadblocks to communication:

1. sending confusing messages by saying one thing and doing something else

2. expecting people always to act a certain way

3. seeing a person or situation differently than someone else

Becoming aware of our own feelings and trying to understand the feelings and views of others is the first step toward good communication. These activities should help you to better understand why communicating with others can be difficult, and they may also help you discover ways to improve relationships with parents and friends.

Assumptions

Objective:
To help students explore the concepts of perceptions and assumptions

Time:
One session

Procedures:
Introduce the topic to students in the following manner:
Sometimes our perception, how we see a situation, plays tricks on us. This is very much like a magician producing popcorn out of a hat. It appears he is popping popcorn in the hat, but of course that is not the case.

Now I am going to describe a situation. Your task will be to tell me what you think has happened. Here is how it works:

I will describe a situation like this: "Mary is scratching her head, therefore..."

When I call on you, you may give an answer like: "I think she doesn't know the answer to a question" or "I believe that she has fleas and they are biting her."

Then I will call on someone and say: "Will you play the role of Mary and tell why you were scratching your head? The answer might be: "I was giving a secret signal to a friend."

If I were to say or believe that Mary did not know an answer or that she had fleas, what problems could result? (Discuss.)

Now let's try these situations: The above procedure may be applied to the following situations:
  a. José is reading a note, therefore...
  b. Amy's face turned red, therefore...
  c. Latasha searched through her purse, therefore...
  d. Kevin looked at Marvin's paper, therefore...
  e. Caitlyn got up and left the room, therefore...
  f. Craig pushed Jane, therefore...
  g. Tom opened Amy's purse, therefore...
  h. Reid was called to the office, therefore...
  i. Lionel glanced at the clock, therefore...
  j. Michael had tears in his eyes, therefore...
  k. Gina giggled, therefore...

Wrap-up: It is easy to observe a situation and say what we *think* is happening. This kind of guesswork can lead us into all kinds of problems involving other people. Students could be encouraged to discuss their own experiences where they ran into a problem through a faulty perception.

E

Verbal and Nonverbal Communications

Objective:
To help students understand various modes of communication

Time:
Two sessions

Materials:
Worksheet

First Session: Introduce activity by stating the concept of communication and its various means

1. Elicit from students a definition of "communication."
2. Brainstorm examples of communication, listing them on chalkboard, e.g.,
   smiling, writing, talking, looking, winking, gesturing, etc.
3. Distribute magazines, newspapers and have students look for examples of specific
   communication situations. Ask them to describe the parts of the communication that are
   nonverbal and the parts that are *verbal*.
4. Classify the examples: nonverbal *vs.* verbal, social *vs.* work, pleasant *vs.*
   unpleasant, or friendly *vs.* unfriendly.
5. Allow time for students to make collages (individual or combined) of the selected examples.

Second Session: Distribute worksheet and allow time for students to complete it.

1. Ask selected students to demonstrate message-sending through pantomime. Select "feeling"
   words from worksheet as assignments, asking students to show how communication may be
   effected through
   a. gestures, i.e., shake hands, open arms
   b. posture, i.e., slump, bouncing walk, straight backed, arms folded
   c. eye movement, i.e., humor, anger, interest, flirtation
   d. clothing, i.e., neat, fancy, sloppy, casual, uniform

2. Ask members of the audience to try and identify the message being sent by each demonstrator
   and write it on a piece of paper.

Personal application:
Can you think of some examples of how your verbal or nonverbal behavior has helped or hindered
communication?

Evaluation:
Ask students how they would act or speak to communicate these messages:
(1) I am interested, (2) Please call on me, I know the answer, (3) I'm bored, (4) That's a stupid/
good idea, and (5) I'm worried/concerned.
 All should plan how to do each response, but call on volunteers.

Feeling Words and Actions

For each of the feeling words listed below, think of some actions you could use to express that feeling, to communicate it to someone else.

Feeling Words   **Feeling Actions**

1. happiness

2. unhappiness

3. anger

4. boredom

5. worry

6. gratitude

7. relaxation

8. relief

9. fear

10. jealousy

Now, pretend you were in a situation that called for you to show each of the above feelings. Pick two feeling words and write a short situation where you would have to communicate that feeling to another person. Describe each situation below.

Situation A:

Situation B:

E

Communication of Feeling Through Body Language

Objective:
To help students understand how body language communicates

Time:
One or two sessions

Materials:
Messages written on slips
of paper, handouts on body language (2 pages)

Procedures:
1. Before the lesson begins, place the messages in a box.
2. Divide the group into two teams. Explain that you are going to play charades. The number one player on the first team is to take a message out of the box, study it briefly, give it to the group's leader or teacher and then try to communicate the message to his or her own team without speaking. Ask the members of the opposing team to remain silent. Each player will be allowed one minute. At the end of one minute, if the player's team has not guessed the message, the other team has one minute to try. Score one point for the team that guesses correctly within the time limit.
3. Next, the number one player from the second team draws a message and the procedure is repeated. The first team to score seven points wins the game.

MESSAGES

I like you.	*I am so ashamed.*	*I am proud.*	*Will you help me?*
I am discouraged.	*I am hurt.*	*I am sad.*	*I am delighted.*
We won!	*I am scared.*	*I don't want to do it.*	*I am furious.*
I am bored.	*I will not give up.*	*Be quiet.*	*I am happy.*
Go away.	(More difficult ones can be added or as replacements)		

4. Discuss:
    a. What are some of the ways you can communicate boredom nonverbally?
    b. Show me how you look when you're excited. Then, how do you look when you're calm?
    c. Remember a time when you were refused something you wanted and so you pouted? How did you look?
    d. Which feelings are easiest for you to communicate nonverbally?
    e. Which feelings do you like to show to others?
    f. Which feelings do you prefer to hide from others?
    g. How do you know when you have communicated your feelings?

5. Distribute handout and let students try out these movements in pairs. If time permits some volunteers can demonstrate a few expressions.

BODY LANGUAGE

Movement	Possible Meaning
Pat on the head	Approval
Lift one eyebrow	Disbelief
Life both eyebrows	Surprise
Lower both eyebrows	Uneasiness or suspicion or anxiety
Slap forehead	Forgetfulness
Wink one eye	Flirtatious or very friendly
Stare	Rudeness or superiority
Closed eyes	Bored and restless, or tense
Eyes and face suddenly look down	Wish to take back what said or did — ashamed
Eyes intensely looking, wrinkled forehead, and downcast look	Reflectiveness
Take off glasses or look away	Wish to not be seen or not to see
Rub nose	Puzzlement
Smile	Happy or apologize
Frown	Unhappy or discontent
Nod head	Agreement
Shake head	Disagreement
Thrust head forward	Aggressiveness
Blank look	Depression
Face suddenly collapses	Guilt
Hunching shoulders	Bored, restless, or tense
Shrug shoulders	Indifference
Pulled in shoulders	Suppressed anger

BODY LANGUAGE (continued)

Movement	Possible Meaning
Raised shoulders	Fear
Square shoulders	Taking on responsibility
Bowed shoulders	Carrying a burden
Tap fingers	Impatience
Clasp arms	Isolate or protect
Steeple fingers.	Superiority
Move hands or play with ring while reading	Anxiety, nervousness, or embarrassment
Fingers doodled and head tilted	Boredom
Clenched fist	Anger
Constant touching	Want for companionship
Height (stand on toes)	Dominance
Stiff and straight posture	Immovable and determined
Listless posture	Depression
Jerky movement	Frustration
Shrinking body movements	Depression
Rocking legs and feet	Tense, bored, or restless
Leg swinging or tapping	Tense, bored, or restless
Restless movement	Anxiety, nervousness, or embarrassment
Sit in the middle of bench	Dominance
Sit on the end of bench	Privacy
Sit to one side of middle	Sharing

Charades

Objective:
To give students an opportunity to practice and interpret nonverbal communication

Time:
One session

Procedures:
Ground rules for the class need to be established.

Suggestions:

1. Two minute time limit.

2. No talking by person giving clues.

3. Use standard clues as established by groups.

Common signs need to be established for the categories:

1. Movie: running a camera.

2. Song: mime singing or make circular motion for record spinning.

3. Book: hold hands in front as if supporting a book.

4. TV Show: put hands up by head to denote rabbit ears.

Students may contribute titles or teacher may have a list made up. Each should be on a separate strip of paper. Students draw a selection and then act out the title to their group.

The game can be scored by awarding one (1) point for each round to the team that solves the clue in the shortest amount of time.

Advisors should encourage all students to take a turn at acting out the title.

F

Decision-Makers

Objective:
To help students learn about types of decision-makers and determine which type they are

Time:
Two sessions

Materials:
"Six Types of Decision-Makers" worksheet

Procedures:

Discuss these words, perhaps putting definition or synonym on board:

dependent:	relying on others' help
scared:	afraid
logical:	using reasoning, not feelings
impulsive:	thoughtless, hasty
procrastinate:	put things off
emotional:	depending on feelings only

Ask students to brainstorm the different ways people solve problems (make decisions)

1. Discuss common ways people solve problems (make decisions).
2. State that people often identify with known types of decision-makers and that it helps you make better decisions to know which "type" you are or are like.
3. Distribute worksheet "Six Types of Decision-Makers."
4. Ask students to complete worksheet and to think about which combination of types would be best at decision making.

Personal application:

Review results of worksheet tasks
Consider the risks and benefits of each style.
Discuss how to deal with someone who represents each of the types.
Ask students to share decisions they have made that were like those of characters.

Six Types of Decision-Makers

All of us at times can identify with each type of decision-maker. Read the description of each type. Check the type if it ever applies to you. List an advantage and a disadvantage for each type.

DEPENDENT DAN ☐

Depends on others to make decisions for him. He thinks others know what is best for him.

Advantage:

Disadvantage:

IMPULSIVE IRMA ☐

Does things without considering choices. She usually doesn't think before acting.

Advantage:

Disadvantage:

SCARED SARAH ☐

Knows there are choices but is scared to make a decision. She worries about the consequences of her decisions.

Advantage:

Disadvantage:

PROCRASTINATNG PETE ☐

Studies choices and gathers lots of information. He doesn't know what is important to him so he has trouble making choices.

Advantage:

Disadvantage:

LOGICAL LARRY ☐

Makes decisions after considering alternatives and consequences. He acts on his decision and changes them when they are no longer satisfactory.

Advantage:

Disadvantage:

EMOTIONAL ELLA ☐

Studies her choices and makes a decision based on her feelings and what's important to her.

Advantage:

Disadvantage:

F

"Not So Simple" Solutions

Objective:
To help students analyze common school-related conflict situations and possible solutions

Time:
One to two sessions

Procedures:

Make a list of problems that often arise in school and put it on the board. Elicit additional ones. Some topics that may be appropriate are listed below.

Suggested Topics

Handling gossip about yourself

Extortion

Someone cheating off your paper

Cutting school

Accused of something you did not do

To tattle or not to tattle

Being bullied

Talking back to teachers

Getting behind in your work

Tardiness to class

Being with someone who gets in trouble

These topics can be discussed, role-played, or written about (one, two or more) as students seek to determine how they might be solved.

F

Shelter

Objective:

To provide an opportunity for students to work together in solving a group problem

Time:

One session
(minimum of 25 minutes)

Materials:

Newspaper stacks, tape,
Process Observer Sheets

Procedures:

The class is divided into groups of five to seven, with an observer in each group. Each group is given a five-inch high stack of newspapers and a roll of tape. The instructions to the students are that they are to plan and build a shelter in which they could all fit inside (including the process observer) using only the newspaper and tape. No other supports such as chairs or walls may be used, but groups may tape their shelter to the floor if so desired.

Total planning and building time for this task is 25 minutes. They may take as much of this time for planning as they wish, but once they start building they may not go back to the planning period. During planning, they may talk but not touch the materials; during the building period, they may touch the materials but not talk. The teacher will announce the time every five minutes. The activity is followed by process observer reports in the small groups and a general discussion.

Variation: Checkerboard:

Each group is given two large pieces of construction paper, one red and one black (other contrasting colors will do), and is asked to design and build a checkerboard. As in Shelter, the group may not touch the materials during the planning or talk during building. Twenty minutes total time should be allowed.

Process Observer Sheet

yes no   Did all the members of your group share in the planning of the shelter?

yes no   During the planning time, did any members of the group touch the materials?

yes no   Did all the members of the group share in the building of the shelter?

yes no   Was there any talking while the building of the shelter was taking place?

yes no   Did any one person assume the leadership role during this process?

yes no   Did the members work well together as a group?

yes no   Were all suggestions listened to with respect within the group?

yes no   Can you think of ways the group could have been more effective?
List your suggestions:

        1.

        2.

3

Group Structure

Objective:
To work as a group toward a common goal

Time:
One or two sessions

Materials:
See below

Materials: Building materials, such as pieces of cardboard, scraps of cloth, yarn, scissors, paper cups, paper plates, sparkles, crepe paper streamers, tape, toothpicks, construction paper, wrapping paper, string, glue. A box for each group of six and enough play money to give each group $100 should be provided.

Procedures:

1. Sort the materials putting an equal collection plus $100 into each box.

2. Divide the class into groups of five or six.

3. Give each group a box of materials.

4. Ask each group to make a structure using the box as base. Structures will be judged on strength and creativity.

5. Explain that students may use their money to buy materials from the other groups. They may also initiate trades.

6. After approximately 20 minutes, stop the activity and allow each group to display its structure.

7. In a large group, discuss:

    a. What did you learn about yourself from this activity?

    b. What did you learn about your group?

    c. How well did your group work together?

F

Cooperation Squares Task

Objectives:
To analyze certain aspects of cooperation in solving a group problem.
To build awareness of some of the participants' own behavior traits.

Time:
One or two sessions

Materials:
Envelopes with puzzle pieces made from the five patterns on the following pages. (Photocopy number of patterns needed.)

Procedures:
1. Large group should be broken into small groups of five participants who are to arrange themselves in discussion circles. Use floor, if possible.
2. Each person in a small group should be given an envelope containing pieces for forming squares.
3. At the signal of the leader, the task of the group is to form five squares of equal size. Each square will be made up of three puzzle pieces. The task is not completed until: (1) everyone has before him a perfect square; (2) all the squares are of the same size; *and* (3) one square of the five has two pieces with the same letter.

     The rules while completing the task are: No one may speak; no member may ask for a card or in any way signal that he wants one; members may give cards to others. Write these rules on the chalkboard or on a sheet of chart paper.
4. When all or most of the groups have finished, call time and have the small groups discuss the experience. Discuss such questions as:

    - *How did you feel when someone held a piece and did not see the solution?*
    - *Why did you feel this way?*
    - *What was your reaction when someone finished his square and then sat back without seeing whether his solution prevented others from solving their problem? Could you have reacted another way? Would this have helped or hindered solving the problem? Why?*
    - *What was your feeling if you finished our square and then began to realize that you would have to break it up and give a piece away? Why did you feel this way?*
    - *Did the climate (the way people acted) help or hinder getting the job done? Why?*

Prepare a set of squares and an instruction sheet for each group of five students. A set consists of five envelopes containing pieces of stiff paper cut into patterns that will form five 6"X6" squares as shown on the attached diagrams.

Several individual combinations will be possible but only one total combination.

Hint: Three of the *B* pieces are identical, therefore to win, a group needs one square with two *B* pieces.

Cut each square into the parts and lightly pencil in the letter A-E. Then mark the envelopes A through E and distribute the pieces thusly: Envelope A: all *A* pieces; Envelope B: all *B* pieces; Envelope C: all *C* pieces; etc.

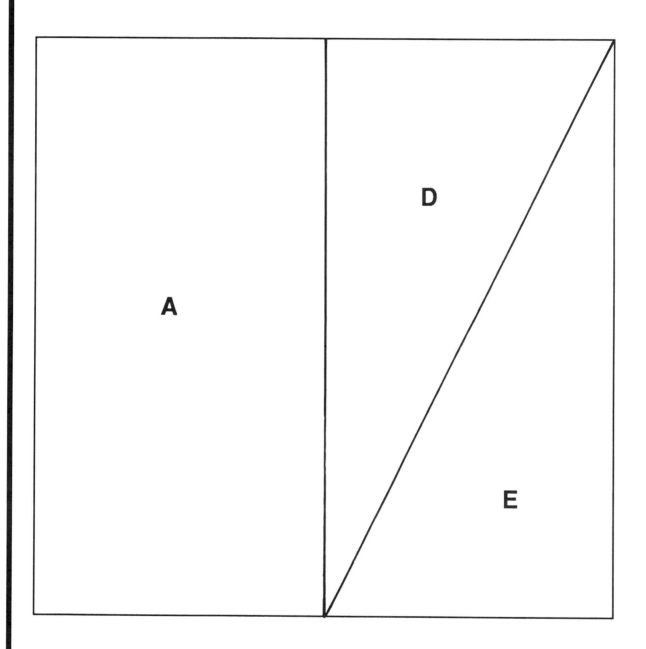

F

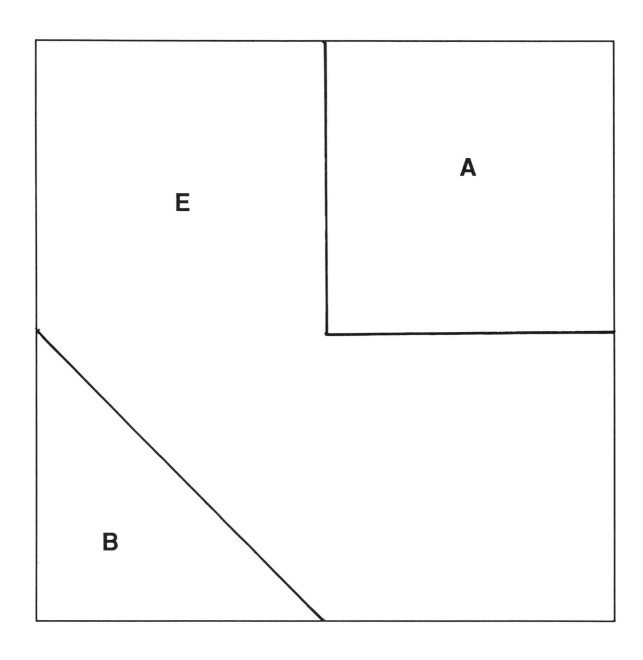

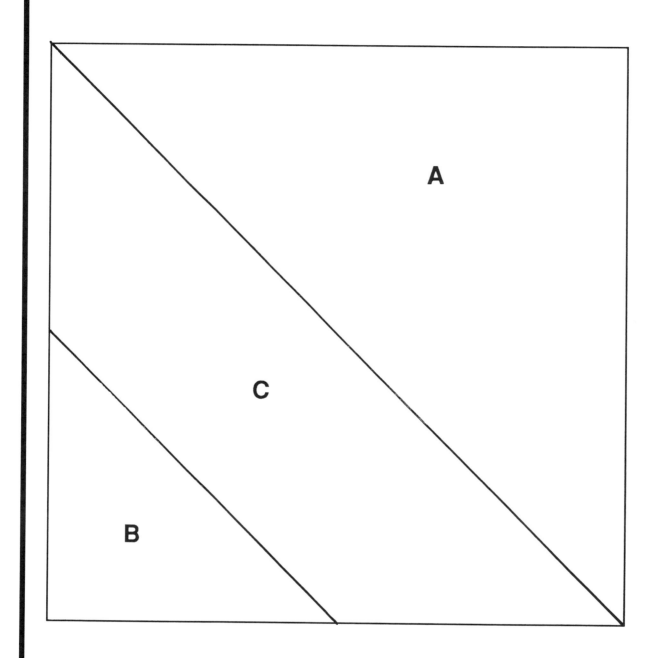

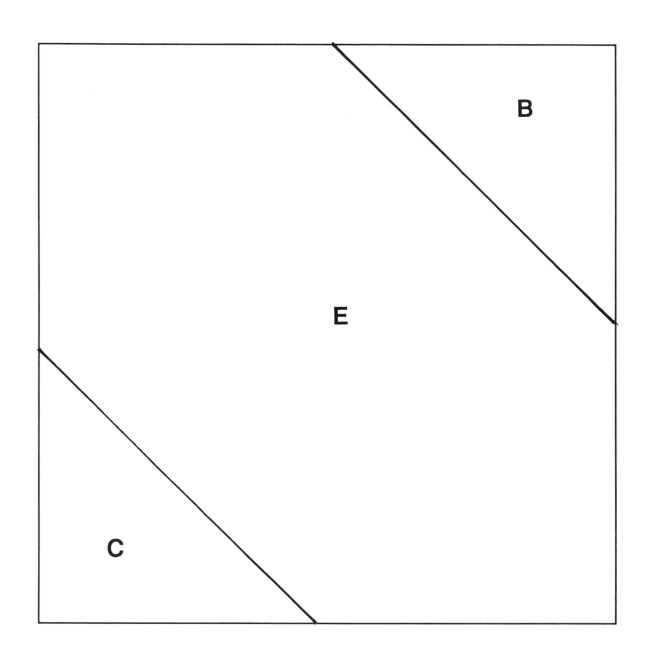

F

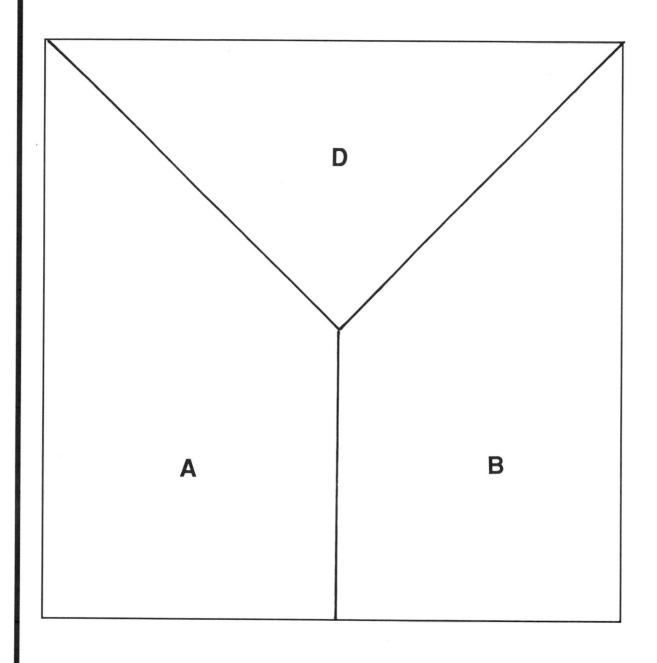

F

Tic-Tac-Toe

Objectives:
To experience one type of leadership and to gain more understanding about communications

Time:
One session

Materials:
Large sheets of paper/pencil for each
of four groups; blindfolds

Procedures:

Groups of four are formed. Within each group, two members are blindfolded; one large piece of paper is placed between them. The other two group members sit near the blindfolded members, each becoming a leader of one of the others. Tic-tac-toe grid is drawn on the paper by a sighted member.

The blindfolded members are instructed to play tic-tac-toe with one another by following the directions of their respective leaders. The leaders may give no physical help to the players who must rely on verbal directions alone. A second game is played, this time with the roles reversed and with the other two players blindfolded; the pairs also change partners for the second game. The whole procedure is repeated in a third and fourth game but now without blindfolds.

Discussion:

1. What feelings did you experience while you were the blindfolded player? Were there any frustrations involved while you were the player? How did you react when having to depend totally upon your leader?

2. What were your feelings while you were leading the blindfolded player? Did you like having that much power? What type of cues was the player communicating to you while you were leading?

3. Did you feel any differences when you played without the blindfold? Were you more or less frustrated by being able to see? Did you agree with the leader's decisions? What effect did the added information have on your responses to the leader?

4. As the leader, did you feel any differences when your player was not blindfolded?

*Circle of Knowledge**

Objective:
To build teamwork and develop friendly competition while learning

Time:
One session

Materials:
Pencil/pen, sheet of paper for each small group.
Chalkboard or overhead for teacher.

1. Introduce the group to the rules for the Circle of Knowledge Activity.

    a. Each group will have five minutes to generate all the knowledge it can on the announced topic.

    b. Each group in turn will be able to present its recorded knowledge, one answer at a time. Each correct answer will score two points. Each incorrect answer, if caught by other teams, will cause a deduction.

    c. If a team thinks another team's answer is incorrect, it may challenge that team. If the challenge is right, the team gets one point, if it is wrong, two points are deducted. If more than one team challenges, the challenges are taken in sequential order.

2. Now announce the topic: e.g. states of the United States of America. Each team has five minutes to list as many states as possible.

3. At the end of five minutes ask team one to call out one state from its list. Record the state on the overhead or chalkboard. Call on each team in turn keeping track of points gained and lost. In case of a tie, you can choose to throw out a tie-breaking challenge to the teams as you see fit.

4. If challenges occur, you are the judge as to whether answers are correct or incorrect.

5. Scores might be kept over a period of time, say, five games and then teams switched to "even" things out. Over a whole year, individual scores could be kept like in rotating bridge and these students can be given special recognition. Or your class could challenge another advisory class to a match.

6. Options: There are plenty of topics to use for the circle of knowledge: Teams in the NFL, names in the class, teachers in school, cities in your county, numbers divisible by 9, etc. After awhile have the students submit suggestions; share them with other teachers.

*Because of the diversity of topics available for this exercise, it can be repeated on a regular basis without boredom.

F

The Penny Game

Objective:
To develop skills required for working in small groups while developing a spirit of friendly competition.

Time:
One session

Materials:
One copy of "Things to Find On A Penny" for each task group and a penny for each person.

Procedures:

1. Break the group into equal teams of 4, 5, or 6 people.
2. Request that each group quickly choose a leader. Leaders should report to you.
3. Give each leader the "Things to Find On A Penny" guide sheet and a penny for each member of the group. Explain that students are to find as many things on the list as they can in a 15 minute time period.
4. Call time and ask groups to exchange papers. Read the correct answers or list on chalkboard if spelling is important. Groups should score the total number right. Announce the winner.
5. If time allows, ask groups to discuss the following:
   1. Would you, as a group, do anything different if you were to play a similar game again? What? Why?
   2. How can a game like this help our group to work better together?

<u>Answers</u>

1.	America	7.	One sent (cent)	13.	In/of
2.	Hair/hare	8.	T	14.	Link
3.	Ted/Bert	9.	Memorial	15.	Eye
4.	United	10.	Rust	16.	Bus
5.	Hair/whisker/ear	11.	Liberty	17.	Lib
6.	Date	12.	Column	18.	One/nite

Things To Find On A Penny

Leader, please read the following to your group:

> Our task is to find as many things as we can from this list on a penny. The things may be words, parts of words, images, etc. Often they will be words meant differently than they are spelled: for example, the answer to a small insect may be the letter "B." We will have 15 minutes.

Now pass out a penny to each group member and work however you choose to get your answers/ recording them on the answer sheet.

1. Name of a song

2. Name of a small animal

3. Two boy's nicknames
   (5 points each)

4. A state of matrimony

5. A part of corn

6. A fruit

7. A messenger

8. A beverage

9. Another name for a religious edifice

10. Another word for corrosion

11. Freedom

12. A line of people

13. Two prepositions

14. Part of a chain

15. Center of a hurricane

16. Means of transportation

17. Women's movement

18. Time of day

Fishbowl — A Role-Playing Activity

Objective:
To enhance students' oral communication skills

Time:
Two sessions

Materials:
Role cards

Procedures:
Prepare role cards as described below. Ask your students to brainstorm a list of topics they feel they could talk about, general topics about which they are all likely to have some knowledge and/or opinions. As they suggest topics, write them on the board.

Then arrange chairs so that six are in the middle, in a circle, and the rest are in a circle on the outside. Ask for volunteers or appoint students to sit in the middle for the first round. Explain to the entire group that you will be passing out role cards to those in the inner circle; these role cards explain the roles these inner circle people are to play. Select one of the topics on the board and announce to the inner circle that topic which they should discuss.

Allow inner circle (fishbowl) students to examine their roles a moment and have them begin. Allow the discussion to continue for several minutes, long enough for each person to play his role. Then have outer circle try to describe or name the role fishbowl students were playing. Discuss how people who enact these roles in real discussions help/hinder the discussion. Then have fishbowl participants rejoin the outer circle.

Repeat with other students in the fishbowl discussing other topics. A chart could be made for students in the outer circle. Down one side could be listed the rules and descriptions of those enacting these roles. Across the top could be listed Group 1, 2, 3, etc. Then, as students in the outer circle guess who is playing each role, they could write names down for that group next to the appropriate role.

Roles:
1. **Initiator:** You help start group, organize, introduce new ideas, keep discussion going and keep members on track.
2. **Dominator:** You won't let anyone else talk. You interrupt, try to get group to listen to you.
3. **Clown:** You make jokes off the topic, show off, disrupt by trying to be funny.
4. **Non-contributing group member:** You say nothing, look bored, do something else at your seat.
5. **Aggressor:** You cut other people down and get angry at them.
6. **Contributing group member:** You listen to others, ask them good questions that show you have listened, and contribute new ideas on the topic.

Directions: As you decide which person is playing each role, write his or her name for that round in the box for that role.

F

The Mystery Game
(a particularly difficult and challenging activity)

Objectives:
To allow students opportunity to analyze communication behavior.
To allow students opportunity to listen to others communicate ideas.
To have students arrange communication in a logical order to solve a problem.

Time:
One session, possibly more

Materials:
A copy of clues for each group

Procedures:

1. The teacher gives the following explanation:

    Today we are going to play a challenging game that will improve your communication skills. Each of the pieces of paper I am holding contains one clue that will help you solve a murder mystery.
    If you put all the facts together, you will be able to solve the mystery. You must find the murderer, the weapon, the time of the murder, the place of the murder, and the motive. Any time you think you know the answers and the group agrees on the guess, you may tell me. I will only tell you whether all five answers are right or wrong. If part of your answers are incorrect, I will not tell you which ones are wrong.

    You may organize yourselves in any way you like. You may not, however, pass your clues around or show them to anyone else, and you may not leave your seats to walk around the group. All sharing of clues and ideas must be done verbally.

2. After clarifying the rules pass out all the clues. Depending on the size of the groups, some individuals may have several clues.

3. Teacher stands back out of the way and may indicate the passing of time. First team to arrive at the correct answers is the winner, but the other team(s) should be allowed to finish on their own.

4. Follow-up:
    Bring class together and analyze communication behavior and breakdowns.
    Possible areas for discussion are: (1) What problems did the group have and how were they solved? (2) What were the reasons for success? (3) Was a leader necessary? (4) What problems arose because some people didn't present their clues? (5) Did anyone ever forget his clue and make an incorrect response?

5. A list of clues and the answer is provided on the next pages. Make copies of the clues and cut them apart for distribution.

The Mystery Game
Clues

When he was discovered dead, Mr. Kelley had a bullet hole in his thigh and a knife wound in his back.

Mr. Jones shot at an intruder in his apartment building at 12:00 midnight.

The elevator operator reported to the police that he saw Mr. Kelley at 12:15 a.m.

The bullet taken from Mr. Kelley's thigh matched the gun owned by Mr. Jones.

Only one bullet had been fired from Mr. Jones' gun.

When the elevator man saw Mr. Kelley, Mr. Kelley was bleeding slightly but did not seem badly hurt.

A knife with Mr. Kelley's blood on it was found in Miss Smith's yard. The knife found in Miss Smith's yard had Mr. Scott's fingerprints on it.

Mr. Kelley had destroyed Mr. Jones' business by stealing all his customers.

The elevator man saw Mr. Kelley's wife go to Mr. Scott's apartment at 11;30 p.m. The elevator man said the Mr. Kelley's wife frequently left the building with Mr. Scott.

Mr. Kelley's body was found in the park at 1:30 a.m. Mr. Kelley had been dead for one hour when his body was found, according to a medical expert.

The elevator man saw Mr. Kelley go to Mr. Scott's apartment at 12:25 a.m. The elevator man went off duty at 12:30 a.m.

It was obvious from the condition of Mr. Kelley's body that it had been dragged a long distance.

Miss Smith saw Mr. Kelley go to Mr. Jones' apartment building at 11:55 p.m.

Mr. Kelley's wife disappeared after the murder; they discovered that he had disappeared.

The elevator man said that Miss Smith was in the apartment building lobby when he went off duty.

Miss Smith often followed Mr. Kelley.

Mr. Jones had told Mr. Kelley that he was going to kill him.

Miss Smith said that nobody left the apartment building between 12:25 a.m. and 12:45 a.m.

Mr. Kelley's blood stains were found in Mr. Scott's car.

Mr. Kelley's blood stains were found on the carpet in the hall outside Mr. Jones' apartment.

ANSWER: After receiving a superficial gunshot wound from Mr. Jones, Mr. Kelley went to Mr. Scott's apartment where he was killed by Mr. Scott with a knife at 12:30 a.m., because Mr. Scott was in love with Mr. Kelley's wife.

G

The Silent Voice

Objective:
To understand the impact and meaning of "first impressions."

Time:
Two sessions

Materials:
"The Silent Voice"
"Lies Around Us"

Procedures:

1. First impressions — what do they tell us? Have students look at "The Silent Voice" and do parts A and B before handing out "Lies Around Us."

2. Hand out "Lies Around Us" and have students complete parts C and D.

The Silent Voice

The way we look … our hair, clothes, and mannerisms all "say things" about us, even in their silence.

A. What do the following statements seem to tell us about a person?

1. She wears pink lace collars and sleeves. She lives in a

2. His hands always look grimy. He works at

3. He walks with bent shoulders and bowed head. He feels

4. Their clothes are always too big for them. They are

5. She chews gum a lot. She cares (or doesn't care) about

6. She always greets people with a smile. She likes to

7. He is always dressed in the latest fashion. He has

B. Look at the lady in the illustration above. From what the "silent voice" is telling you, describe this lady.

Lies Around Us

C. What is this? My secret X-ray vision tells me the little lady in The Silent Voice is not what she seems to be! Describe (in light of this new evidence) what she really is.

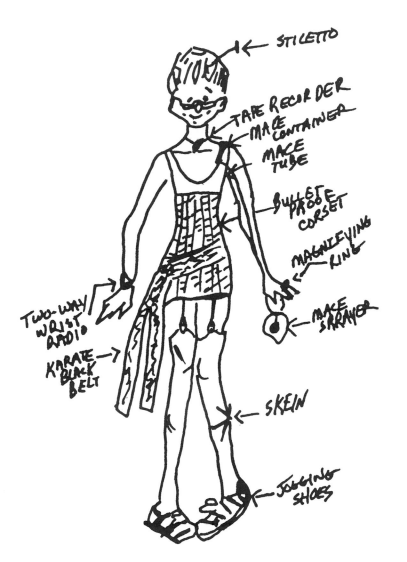

STILETTO

TAPE RECORDER

MACE CONTAINER

MACE TUBE

BULLET PROOF CORSET

MAGNIFYING RING

TWO-WAY WRIST RADIO

KARATE BLACK BELT

MACE SPRAYER

SKEIN

JOGGING SHOES

D. We have just seen that "The Silent Voice" is not always correct. Let's look at some physical characteristics which are "said" to have special meanings. Indicate the common feeling about each. Supply others in blank spaces.

  receding chin

  red hair

  "buck teeth"

  weak handshake

  low voice

  high forehead

E. Describe a situation in which you were surprised to find that someone did not fit the role which the "silent voice" had suggested.

F. Write a story in which persons possessing most of the physical characteristics in "D" actually have the opposite attributes.

G

Friendly Facts

Objective:
To help students realize the importance of friendship in our lives

Time:
Two sessions

Materials:
"Learning About Friends" - teacher copy
Handout: "What Would You Do?"

Procedures:

1. Read "Learning About Friends" to students.

2. Have students complete "What Would You Do?"

3. Discuss student responses.

G

Learning About Friends

Learning about friends begins very early in life. From the time we are born, we all need contact with others. Babies cry for attention as well as for food. They need to be picked up and cuddled. They need to hear the sound of human voices.

When infants receive love and care, they learn to trust others. Babies feel safe knowing that other family members will feed them when they are hungry and comfort them when they are frightened. The warmth, love, and trust that children learn from these first human contacts can set the tone for later friendships. From the family, a child learns how people relate to one another.

As a teenager, you probably feel a special need for someone to talk to. You may be adjusting to a changing body and to changing emotions as well. Friends your own age are going through the same changes, and older friends have already gone through them. They are in a good position to know how you feel.

The need to share feelings and experiences goes beyond the teen years. When you start your first full-time job or move into your first apartment, it will be helpful to know others who are starting out on their own or who have done what you are doing. The need for this kind of friendship will continue throughout your life.

═══════════════════

Have students read and respond to "What Would You Do?" Discuss the different answers students give as solutions to the case studies. Relate these answers to friendships and how we deal with friends.

What Would YOU Do?

How do you react when you face a difficult or unfamiliar problem?
Below each problem, write what you would do in each of the following situations.

Problem One: When you get home from school, you discover that you don't have your keys. The doors are locked and no one is at home. You need to get in so that you can change clothes, have something to eat, and get your basketball. Several friends are waiting for you at the neighborhood park. The game won't start until you arrive. What do you do?

Problem Two: You and a friend are shopping in a local department store. Your friend is in a hurry. Suddenly you hear a loud noise behind you. When you turn around, you see that an elderly man has fallen down. He appears to be badly hurt. No adults are nearby. What do you do?

Problem Three: On Monday morning you realize that the $10 you have isn't enough to pay for the things you want to buy during the week. You need to buy school lunches, a notebook and pen, and a birthday present for your little brother. You've also promised to give a dollar to the muscular dystrophy fund, and you're hoping to buy a new record by your favorite group. In addition, you and your friends usually go out for hamburgers and milkshakes at least once during the week. What do you do?

Problem Four: The teenager who just moved in next door started attending your school this week. You've invited the newcomer to go with you and your friends to a school game this weekend. Your parents are pleased about the invitation. However, before you have a chance to tell your best friend about the plan, he or she tells you how unpleasant the new student seems to be. What do you do?

What's Your Problem?

Objective:
To have students examine the qualities of friendship

Time:
Two sessions

Materials:
"What's Your Problem" teacher copy

Procedures:

1. Read "What's Your Problem?" to students.

2. Discuss:

    a. Put the following on the board and explain why each of these qualities is valuable in a friend. **Loyalty, Reliability, Tolerance;**
    b. What does it mean to "get outside yourself" when listening to someone? What other responsibilities does a good listener have?
    c. How can talking things over help a friendship? Why is this sometimes difficult to do?
    d. Which quality of a friend do you think is the most important?

3. Do the extra activity on the worksheet, if time allows.

G

What's Your Problem?

Dear Nancy,

I have a problem with my friend Juan. We work on the school newspaper together and have been friends for a long time. He joined the soccer team not too long ago and has been acting weird ever since. But last weekend was the worst.

We were supposed to go to the movies Saturday afternoon. When I stopped by Juan's house, his mother said that he had gone to a barbecue with some of the kids from the soccer team. I couldn't believe he didn't even call to let me know!

Then at school on Monday, one of the soccer crowd came up and said, "So, how's Maria?" Maria is my older sister's friend. Juan is the only person who knew I liked Maria, and he promised not to tell anyone else.

I found Juan after math class on Monday and asked him where he got off telling his new friends something he'd promised to keep a secret. And that on top of going to the barbecue with them instead of to the movies with me!

He acted really sorry and embarrassed. It seems he was so excited about being invited to the barbecue that he forgot about going to the movies with me. He said that my secret slipped out because he was nervous about being with those other kids.

I can understand Juan wanting to be friends with this group, because they're the most popular crowd in school. But that doesn't mean that Juan should break his promise to me.

Juan and I used to have some good times together. Maybe I could forget about his skipping the movies, but I feel I can't trust him anymore. Should I stay friends with him?

A Confused,
Eric

Extra Activity

Role play some problems that may occur among friends. Have students volunteer for this if they want to — give some time for brief planning and then have them do the role play.

Friendship Hotline

Objective:
To have students look at friendships and the problems they can present.

Time:
Two sessions

Materials:
"Friendship Hotline" handout

Procedures:

1. Distribute student copies of "Friendship Hotline" handout.

2. Have students work in pairs or small groups and discuss each of the four letters.

3. Each group should have an answer or suggestion for each letter.

4. Have students share answers and discuss responses.

Friendship Hotline

Imagine that you are the author of a newspaper advice column called "Friendship Hotline."
The writers of the following letters are having problems. What advice would you give them?
Use a separate sheet of paper for your answers.

Dear Friendship Hotline,

Lynne and I have been best friends for three years, but so far this year she hasn't wanted to spend much time with me. She has a whole new group of friends. Lynne and I used to ride on the school bus together and do things after school, but she is always with her new group now. Lynne and I were best friends for so long that I lost contact with my old friends. Besides, I don't want to be friends with anyone but Lynne. This is making me very unhappy. What should I do?

Worried

Dear Friendship Hotline,

My problem is that ever since I transferred to a new middle school I've been making up stories to impress the other kids. I don't mean to lie, but sometimes I do it anyway. Once in a while people act as if they believe me, but usually they aren't impressed.

My real goal is to make some friends here, but everybody seems to belong to a group already.

Should I keep on trying to impress people with invented stories? Or is there some other way to get people to accept me?

Bothered.

Dear Friendship Hotline,

My mother doesn't like my group of friends. Whenever I bring some friends home with me, she comes up with a list of complaints about the way they look and act. And if I want to go anywhere with them, she won't let me go, or else she gives me so many rules that I don't have fun.

I guess I could quit going around with the people Mom doesn't like, but I'd rather not do that. What do you think I should do?

Confused

Dear Friendship Hotline,

Some of my friends have started going out on dates, but I haven't. Sometimes this makes me feel lonely and left out.

I like boys, especially one boy who's a grade ahead of me at school. My problem is that I feel uncomfortable around boys, and I say stupid things or else I can't think of anything to say at all.

One idea I had was to write a note to the boy I like at school to tell him how I feel. Would that be a good idea? What should I do to solve my problem?

Lonely

The Positive Response Game

Objective:

To become aware of ways people respond to each other.

Time:

One session

Procedures:

Begin the session by saying that today we're going to play the positive response game. Explain that the positive response game is played by everyone but that it primarily involves the area of boy-girl relationships. Tell them that it's just a fact of life that all boys and all girls are involved in trying to get members of the opposite sex to respond positively — to say they like you or to go with you or just to smile and respond positively in some way. Explain that we all need that, and yet, it would really be scary to go up to someone and say, 'I like you, do you like me?' for fear of being told, 'No, I don't like you.' Most of us could not handle being told that directly, so we come up with all kinds of clever ways to get people to give us a positive response without our taking a big risk by coming right out and asking.

Continue along these lines:
"Today I'd like you to think of all the ways you know that people do this. Maybe this is the way you get a positive response from a boy or girl, or a way that you have noticed that a boy or girl tries to get you to respond in a nice way, or some way that a friend of yours does it. Let's make a list of as many ways as we can that boys and girls try to get positive responses from each other."

Following the introduction, they should really be ready to talk honestly about the response game. Encourage them to tell their stories. You might go first — telling of a way in which you have gotten members of the opposite sex to respond positively to you.

After the students have shared their stories, explain to them that there is nothing wrong with beating around the bush instead of coming right out with whatever they want to say or do. Sometimes it's much smarter, because the risk involved in coming right out and asking for affection is really too great. An excellent discussion topic to follow this up is "One way I draw attention to myself."

If the group responds well to the activity, you might wish to expand the topic by using the discussion topics listed on the following page. Starred items are particularly appropriate.

G

POSITIVE RESPONSE GAME (continued)

*How to get attention from the opposite sex.
A time when someone had a crush on me.
A boy (girl) I would like to speak to but am afraid to.
A time I revealed my feelings for another.
A time I was with a member of the opposite sex and didn't know what to say.
A time a boy (girl) said something to me and I was embarrassed.
A time I wish I hadn't told a boy (girl) something.
A time when I was the only boy (girl).
A time I was embarrassed when I was with my boyfriend (girlfriend).
A time I wanted to date, but my parents wouldn't let me.
How my parents react to my boyfriend (girlfriend).
A time I was supposed to act like a "man" (lady) because I was a boy or girl.
A time I acted tough to impress my boyfriend (girlfriend).
My best feature is ...
My worst feature is...

*What I think people notice first about me.
  A time when I felt all eyes were on me.
*A time I thought I looked nice and someone told me I didn't.
  A time I really looked bad and something important happened.
  A time I didn't want my picture taken.
  A time that I was very self-conscious about my appearance.
  A time someone's physical appearance influenced my opinion of him/her.

*Why physical appearance is or isn't important to me.
*Why I wish I was taller, shorter, thinner.
*If I could change one thing about the way I look.
  One thing I have improved about my appearance.
*One thing about me I could improve and haven't.
  Something I want to change about myself but can't.
  How I react to a person's severe physical handicap.
  Something about the way I look that used to bother me but doesn't now.

Questions On Tolerance

Objective:
To explore the concept of tolerance toward other people.

Time:
One session

Procedures:

1. Initiate discussion on tolerance. Give examples of intolerance.
    a. What does "tolerance" mean?
    b. Do you think you are more tolerant or less tolerant than you were a year ago?
    c. Are you more tolerant or less tolerant than your parents, brothers, or sisters?

2. Ask students to react to questions from the list on the left below.
3. Use additional topics on the right if time and interest warrant their use.
4. Make up any other questions that seem appropriate. For an additional activity, have class members brainstorm ways they could change themselves to become more tolerant.

How many of you:
1. like the color orange?
2. like shoulder-length hair on boys?
3. like long hair on girls?
4. think it's OK to smoke?
5. would vote for a woman president?
6. think it's OK for men to cry?
7. think it's OK for women to cry?
8. would share your lunch with a black person?
9. think that Japanese know karate best?
10. think Italians make the best pizzas?
11. think that most Italians are gangsters?
12. think Catholic schools are stricter than public schools?
13. think long-haired people are hippies?
14. think it's OK for a woman to be a truck driver?
15. think women should be assigned to combat units?
16. would marry someone of a different race or religion?
17. think fat people have a better sense of humor?
18. think people with Southern accents are hillbillies?
19. think women are worse drivers than men?

Because of one or two people, I hated the whole group.
A time my prejudice or intolerance got in the way.
Something I just cannot tolerate.
How I deal with intolerance or prejudice in an older person.
A time an adult was more prejudiced than me.
A time I became friends with someone everyone else was against.
How I deal with intolerance or prejudice against me.
A time I helped a friend become less prejudiced.
A time someone was different but it didn't matter.
A time I was tolerant of someone's ideas.

G

Putting It All Together

Objective:
To improve students' knowledge of communication skills by applying them in role-played, simulated situations.

Time:
Several sessions

Materials:
"Putting It All Together!"
"Message Slips" worksheets
Evaluation Questionnaire

Procedures:

First Session
1. Divide students into groups of about five each. Hand each of the groups the "Putting It All Together!" worksheet, which has a number of role-play situation suggestions on it. Ask them to prepare a skit based on an assigned (or selected) numbered situation on the worksheet. Allow ten minutes for the preparation of the skit.

2. Allow groups to present skits. Have "audience" identify specific features of interpersonal communication that were shown: verbal and nonverbal elements, message, sender, receiver, feedback, roadblocks, etc.

3. Cut up message slips ("Message Slips" worksheet) and distribute to class. Have students work in pairs to present the idea on a message slip to the class. The "audience" must guess which message is being sent. They may use the summary sheet on "Putting It All Together!" worksheet for hints.

4. Distribute evaluation sheets. Have students complete them.
Discuss what has happened in these sessions, asking students to share their ideas about the activities, how it helped them in school, what they liked, didn't like about particular activities, e.g., the IMP.

Evaluation:
Evaluation Questionnaire
Role-play performances
Competed IMP's and informal comments

Putting It All Together

I. Vocabulary Review: Can you define or give an example of each word?

interpersonal	communication	receiver
friendly behavior	verbal	feedback
characteristics	nonverbal	active listening
relationships	sender	roadblocks

II. Role-play Situations: Pick one of these situations and make up a skit that shows communication taking or not taking place

1. Let a classmate know you would like to be friends.

2. Let someone know you are angry with him/her.

3. Help someone you don't know in an unfamiliar place, e.g., store, bus.

4. Show others you don't like the way they are behaving.

5. Show that you don't want to be disturbed.

6. Show that you are confident, comfortable in front of a group.

7. Say "no" to something your friends are trying to get you to do.

8. Show that you are pleased and happy with something.

9. Ask a parent an important question or favor.

10. Explain something to a teacher.

III. Guessing the message: Which of these messages is being role-played?

I'm glad to meet you.	I'm nervous.	I'd like to meet you.
I'm so excited.	My ____ hurts.	I'm tired.
I'm bored.	I'm proud of my work.	I'm not interested.
I don't understand.	I feel terrific today.	I disapprove of what
I'm so confused, lost!.	You're late.	you are doing.

Message Slips

Cut on dotted lines and give to students

I'm glad to meet you.	I'm tired.
I'm so excited.	I'm so angry with you for being late.
I'm bored.	I'm impatient.
I'm worried.	I'm in love.
I'm nervous.	I'm not interested.
eye tooth My foot hurts ear	I can't see well.
I'm proud of my work.	I have a question I don't understand.
I'd like to meet you.	I need help.
Ouch, that's hot!	I'm so confused, lost.
I feel terrific today!	I'm really interested!

Interpersonal Relationships Evaluation

Directions: Pick the best answers for problems 1-4. Circle your choices.

1. **The best definition for good communication is:**
   a. sending a message to another person
   b. telling another person a message
   c. getting a message across to another person so that it is understood as you meant it to be

2. **Pick the way or ways that people communicate with each other:**
   a. write a letter
   b. talk to a friend
   c. motion to someone to approach you
   d. wink at your best friend
   e. all of the above.

3. **Communication has four basic parts or elements. They are:**
   a. sender, receiver, message, feedback
   b. radio, receiver, message, frequency
   c. people, message, words, meaning
   d. radio, television, telephone, telegraph
   e. none of the above

4. **"Feedback" is a word used when we talk about communication. Pick the best definition for feedback.**
   a. give information to someone else
   b. reaction from the receiver that shows he/she got the message
   c. provide "feed" or food to someone
   d. all of the above

5. **Circle three nonverbal ways of communication in the list below:**
   a. adult in police uniform
   b. whisper
   c. sing a song
   d. wink
   e. telephone message
   f. frown

6. You have lived on your street for five years and have been friends with several boys and girls on your street during that time. A new house has been built recently and sold to a family having two children — one in the fifth grade and one in the seventh grade. Both of the children seem to be shy and have not played with you or your friends since moving in about three weeks ago. So far you have said "Hi" to them and they have answered "Hi" back to you. **List three verbal behaviors and three nonverbal behaviors that you could use to make them feel more comfortable.**
   Verbal:

   Nonverbal:

7. **Circle the letter in front of the four skills that open and maintain effective communication with others.**
   a. ask questions
   b. yell at others when you think they are wrong
   c. give advice and criticism
   d. avoid argument
   e. use friendly body language
   f. reflect meanings
   g. lean away from others when talking

8. Some people cut off communication by blaming others. **List three verbal and three nonverbal behaviors of a blamer.**

   Verbal:

   Nonverbal:

9. The four common types of roadblockers are the blamer, the computer, the pleaser, and the distractor. **Identify which type of roadblocker would make the statements given below:**
   a. "It is 692.3 miles from our house to the beach."
   b. "You are a dumb somebody."
   c. "Gee, you're always right."
   d. "I want to go to the — hey, there's a hair on your shoulder."
   e. "We need $22^{3/4}$ sandwiches for the party."
   f. "You should have known that you couldn't do that job."

10. Making and keeping friends require certain behaviors. List three behaviors that you find helpful in making and keeping friends. **Then, list three behaviors that are not helpful in making and keeping friends.**

    Helpful:

    Not helpful:

11. A classmate gives you a piece of cake from his/her lunch. You like this friendly behavior and wish to show your feelings. What can you say and to to show how you feel? **List your responses below.**

12. Label each part of the communication process, and fill in the correct information.

    _____   _____   _____

    _____   _____

    Lonzy says to Arnetta, "I like your hair." She smiles and says, "Thank you."
    a. message   b. sender   c. receiver   d. feedback-verbal   e. feedback-nonverbal

Part II

Activities

Third Year

Contents III

NOTE: numbers in parentheses indicate number of related handouts

Crazy, Mixed-up Advisor

Objective:
To help students understand the role of the advisor

Time:
One session

Materials:
"Crazy Mixed-up Advisor worksheet

Procedures:

TO THE ADVISOR: This activity is to be presented as a competition. Tell the group that
 the object of the activity is to unscramble the scrambled words in all of the "Crazy Mixed-up
Advisor" statements. The person who finishes first is to stand up and say: "You're a crazy
mixed-up advisor." He/she is then to bring his/her sheet to you for checking. If he/she has
unscrambled all correctly, he/she wins. If he/she misses any or unscrambles them incorrectly,
then you are to call him/her a "Crazy Mixed-up Advisee," and the game continues until a
student guesses all correctly.

ANSWERS

1. responsibility
2. grades
3. goals
4. listen
5. peers/teachers
6. report card
7. advisory
8. parents
9. folder
10. qualities
11. activities
12. learn
13. myself
14. opinions
15. teacher
16. questions
17. decisions
18. friend

CRAZY MIXED-UP ADVISOR

1. My advisor is concerned about my _____ and my progress in school.
   d r e s g a

2. My advisor will help me set some personal _____
   o s l a g

3. My advisor will _____ if I have a problem with school, classes, or friends.
   n e t s i l

4. My advisor can help me learn how to develop positive relationships with _____ and _____
   r p e e s   h r e e c t a s

5. My advisor will give me my _____ _____
   p r e t r o   a d r c

6. My advisor will introduce me to other students in _____
   v i d a r o s y

7. My advisor will answer my _____ questions about school.
   r a n p e s t

8. My advisor will keep my advisory _____ so I can see it.
   l o r f e d

9. My advisor will tell me about the good _____ he/she sees in me.
   s a i l e q u i t

10. My advisor can help me decide which _____ to participate.
    c i v a t i e t i s

11. My advisor can help me figure out which ways I _____ best
    a r n e l

12. My advisor can help me understand _____ better.
    s m e l f y

13. My advisor will listen to my _____ and ideas about out school.
    n o o n s i i p

14. My advisor will talk to me if I have a problem with another student or a _____
    h a c e r t e

15. My advisor can help me learn to make _____.
    s n i d o s i c e

16. Maybe my advisor might even turn out to be a _____
    n e f i r e

Acting vs. Thinking Behaviors

Objective:
To help students know appropriate school behaviors and be able to distinguish between *acting* and *thinking* behaviors

Time:
Two sessions

Materials:
Worksheet on Acting/Thinking Behaviors

Procedures:

1. Share definitions of acting and thinking behaviors
    acting behavior: behavior that others can see
    thinking behavior: behavior that cannot be seen, but may be inferred,
                                         guessed at by others, e.g.,daydreaming.

2. Review concept: Behavior is what we do.
3. What behaviors go on in a typical class? Ask students to look around them and pick examples of behavior that they see in other students.
4. List examples on the chalkboard: writing, reading, thinking, looking, smiling, frowning, fidgeting, walking, talking.
5. Indicate which behaviors are *acting,* which are *thinking* in the above list.
6. Ask members of the class to role play:

    The class clown   An angry parent
    A bookworm   A person who is lost
    A new person in class

    Discuss, after each role play:
                  What acting behaviors did the person show?
                  What thinking behaviors could you infer or guess?
                  Are there thinking behaviors that you can't infer?

7. Discuss the following as a way of bringing closure:
    a. Can people usually tell what you're thinking by your behavior.
    b. When is it helpful to know what people are thinking?
    c. Which is easier to control, acting or thinking behavior?

Judging Acting and Thinking Behaviors

Instructions: The following behaviors can best be described as either ACTING or THINKING behaviors. After each behavior place either an "A" if it is an ACTING behavior or a "T" if it is a THINKING behavior.

1. Cigarette smoking

2. Remembering a movie you saw.

3. Running to class

4. Talking yourself out of asking for a new bicycle

5. Asking to go to the mall with friends

6. Daydreaming about next summer

7. Getting upset over something dumb you said

8. "Re-living" an accident you once had

9. Telling yourself to slow down and relax

10. Buying a shirt at Sears

11. Having a daydream about becoming President

12. Yelling at your sister

13. Multiplying 7 x 36 in your head

14. Getting excited about a holiday

15. Eating that 3rd piece of pie

"Hi, my name is ..." or "Let's get acquainted"

Objective:
To help students become acquainted with others in their advisory group (or class)

Time:
One session

Procedures:

Advisor will get students settled, let them choose their own seats.
Advisor introduces him/herself, then explains:

"In advisory we want to learn each others' names as rapidly as possible. To begin
we are going to take turns around the room. Say "hi," share your name and then tell us your
favorite food. After each person says those things I want the whole group together to say
 "Hi, John" (or whatever the student's name is). Then the next person will take his/her turn.

Advisor will start by doing as he/she asked students to do and then students will share
information with the group.

A

Public Interviews

Objective:
To provide an opportunity for students to share values in a non-threatening environment

Time:
One or two sessions

Materials:
Public Interview Questions (2 pages)

Procedures:

1. Ask for student to volunteer to be interviewed.

2. State ground rules:

   a. Volunteer sits in front of the room. (Some students may be more comfortable in their seats.)
   b. Advisor asks questions from the back of the room.
   c. Questions are about values and life.
   d. Volunteer must answer honestly.
   e. Volunteer may "pass" on any question he/she does not wish to answer.
   f. Volunteer may end interview at any time by saying, "Thank you for the interview."

3. Ask questions of volunteer. (Some possible questions are attached.)

4. This procedure may be repeated with new volunteers answering the same questions.

5. It is important for the advisor and peer group to show interest in the advisee's answers.

6. Choose questions which will allow volunteer to explore his/her values.

7. Be careful not to make judgmental comments; remind students about avoiding killer statements.

PUBLIC INTERVIEW QUESTIONS

1. Do you like to take long walks? What are your favorite places?

2. Do you watch TV? What is your favorite program?

3. How do you feel about grades in school?

4. What kind of toothpaste do you use?

5. How do you deal with the unpleasant aspects of school?

6. What are you saving money for?

7. Do you buy many records? What kind?

8. How do you spend your time after school?

9. What magazines do you read regularly?

10. Have you seen any movies in the last few months which you liked? What were they?

11. What are your favorite sports?

12 What do you like best about school?

13. What do you like least about school?

14. Do you have a hobby?

15. How did you get interested in your hobby?

16. Are there some adults outside of school and your family whom you admire? Why?

17. Is there something you want badly but can't afford right now? What?

18. Of all the people you know who have helped you, who has helped the most? How did he/she go about it?

19. Where did you spend the best summer of your life?

20. What one thing would you change about yourself if you could?

21. Do you wear seat belts?

22 How do you feel about going steady?

23. How do you feel about smoking?

(continued)

24. If you had an extra $500 given to you with no strings attached, what would you do with it?

25. Describe the best teacher you ever had.

26. Which celebrity would you like to have for a friend?

27. What is your favorite color?

28. Do you have a favorite food?

29. Do you ever cook? What do you cook?

30. What present would you like to get?

31. Do you ever do things just because others expect you to do them?

32. If someone embarrassed you, what would you do?

33. Would you tell your best friend that he/she has bad breath?

34. Do you get an allowance? Is it big enough?

35. What are three things you are good at?

36. What is the dumbest gift you've ever received?

37. What makes your best friend your best friend?

38. How many people are in your immediate family?

39. What would you suggest to make this a better school?

40. What did you have for breakfast?

41. What is your favorite dessert?

42. What kind of work would you like to do after you graduate?

Closure

1. Discuss with students how they feel being the center of attention and sharing their own values.

2. Ask those who were just listening if they learned something new about the interviewee.

Master—Robot

Objective:
To experience a variety of degrees of control and become aware of reactions of behavioral control.

Time:
One or two sessions

Procedures:

Arrange desks to provide a large arc with room to move about.

Middle schoolers have difficulty observing and checking their own behavior. This activity gives them a chance to be controlled and to control, while experiencing all the levels in between.

1. Tell the students that you want them to be robots while you play the role of the Master Computer.

2. For one minute you should assume control, dictating just what your student-robots will do. (stand, sit, take two steps forward, face the rear, etc.)

3. Next, lift some control and explain that they are no longer robots but they are free to do what they want for one minute as long as they have arms locked with two other people.

4. Then, tell them they are free for one minute as long as they have hands behind their necks, with the use of only one foot.

5. Finally, let students, with your reasonable but necessary limits, be totally free for one minute. Most do not know what to do first.

6. Return to robots.

7. Follow this up with a sharing session where students tell what they felt during the activity.

Variation: Have students select partners. Let them act out Master-Robot roles with the partner for assigned time periods.

Follow up with a talk session.

B

Interpersonal Management Plan

Objective:

Student will develop an Interpersonal Management Plan to improve/change at least one
interpersonal behavior

Time:

Three sessions over
several weeks plus some
individual conferences

Materials:

Interpersonal Management Plan (5 pages)

Procedures:

1. Discuss the term *interpersonal relationship* and how it applies to behaviors at school and
    elsewhere (interpersonal relationships: the way you get along with other people,
    verbal and nonverbal behavior)

2. Elicit examples from students of interpersonal relationships they could work on or change.

3. Distribute IMPs and explain that for the next few weeks each student will have the task of
    trying to improve or change an interpersonal behavior.

4. Demonstrate how Page 1 of the IMP is to be completed using an example "made up" from
    examples given.

5. Have students complete Page 1 of their IMPs, through Step 1.

Allow time for students to talk with teacher-advisor privately about completing Step 2.
Plan quiet activity, reading or quiet games, so that these conferences can be accomplished.

Interpersonal Management Plan

_____   _____
Student's Name   Advisor's Name

OBJECTIVE: You will develop an interpersonal management plan to improve at least one of your interpersonal behaviors.

Step 1: Look at the two lists of interpersonal behaviors. Some are things that you may do; some are things others may do to you. Put OK beside two things that you feel OK about. Then put a check beside two things that you don't feel OK about.

Things I Would Like To Do Or Improve On	Things Others Do To Me
___ smile more	___ smile at me
___ talk to kids I don't know	___ talk to me
___ help others	___ give me help
___ listen to others	___ listen to me
___ answer questions	___ teachers call on me in class
___ talk to teacher(s) after class	___ others call me names
___ avoid calling others names	___ others get in fights with me
___ avoid getting in fights	___ others "push me around" (make me do things that I don't want to do)
___ avoid "pushing others around" (making others do things that they don't want to do)	

Did you put two OK's and two checks on the lists? Now you are ready to start working on your Interpersonal Management Plan. Follow Steps 2 and 3.

Step 2: Select a behavior from the lists that you would like to try to improve.
Write it on the line below.

_____   _____
(Behavior I want to try to improve)   (Advisor's signature and date)

Discuss with your advisor the behavior that you chose for your Interpersonal Management Plan. Your advisor will sign your sheet after your discussion.

Step 3: Complete assignment sheets A, B, C, & D. Have your advisor sign this form after you complete each assignment.

	Completion date	Advisor's Signature
Worksheet A		
Worksheet B		
Worksheet C		
Worksheet D		

A.
Picking A Model — Interpersonal Relationships

Name _____

Behavior you are working on _____

Directions: Your task for this worksheet is to look around you at school or in the community and see if there is someone who has the skill you are working on. It can be a real person — a friend, schoolmate, someone in your advisory group, a teacher or other adult. Or, it can be someone you read about or saw on TV. This person is your MODEL. A model is someone you can copy or try to be like. Fill in the blanks below with the information about your model

_____
       (Model's name)

I have seen this person do a good job using the behavior that I am working on. This is what he/she does and says.

The consequences of my model's behavior are:

Why did you select this model?

Discuss what you have written with your advisor. Your advisor will sign your record sheet.

B.
Making My Plan — Interpersonal Relationships

Behavior you are working on:

Your model:

Discuss with your advisor things you could do to change this behavior. Answer these questions:

How long do you think this will take?

Who might help you?

How might they help you?

What can your advisor or counselor do to help?

What can you do yourself?

Now, make your plan for changing your behavior below.

C.

LOG SHEET — WEEK 3

_____   **BEHAVIOR** _____
(Student's name)

I tried my plan_____
                              (where, when)

Here's what I did:

The consequences were:

                                        _____
                                        (Advisor's signature and date)

LOG SHEET — WEEK 4

_____   **BEHAVIOR** _____
(Student's name)

I tried my plan_____
                              (where, when)

Here's what I did:

The consequences were:

                                        _____
                                        (Advisor's signature and date)

D.
Assessing My Results — Interpersonal Relationships

Name _____

Behavior I worked on_____

My Model(s)_____

DIRECTIONS: Review Worksheets A & B and answer these questions.

I picked an interpersonal behavior that I wanted to work on.	Yes	No
I picked someone who had the skill I was working on, a **model**	Yes	No
I described what the **model** did that I could copy.	Yes	No
I wrote a plan for working on the behavior, an Interpersonal Management Plan	Yes	No
I tried out my plan for _____ weeks My plan was successful.	Yes	No

Some problems I had in carrying out my plan were:

Some things I did really well in carrying out my plan were:

If your plan worked, congratulations! You have successfully carried out your Interpersonal Management Plan.

If your plan didn't work, look at Worksheet C and see if there is something you could change in your plan to help make it work. Get another IMP form from your advisor and start another plan.

OR

You and your advisor may decide that this is a behavior you just can't change at this time. If so, pick another behavior to work on and begin another IMP with Worksheet A.

c

Letter From a Parent

Objective:
To focus students' attention on parental expectations and concerns

Time:
One session

Materials:
"Letter From a Parent" handout

Procedures:

1. Distribute "Letter From a Parent" and read aloud to students. After reading ask students to underline the last sentence in Paragraph 2; the first and last sentence of Paragraph 3; the fourth, sixth and last sentence of Paragraph 4; the fourth sentence of Paragraph 5; and the last sentence in the letter.

2, Say: "These are the things this parent wants for his or her child — let's review them." (You may call on students to identify these wants.) "In the first three sentences of the last paragraph the parent is giving instructions to the child. What are they? Do you think all parents want these things for their child? Does every adolescent want or need the things this parent wants for his/her child?"

LETTER FROM A PARENT

Dear _____,

Every day I see you grow a little, and while I'm really excited about your growing up, I'm a little scared, too.

You've changed a lot from the little kid I once could pick up and hold in my arms when you were frightened or when you were too close to something or someone who might hurt you. I could protect you so easily then. But now you have so many friends and you go so many places, I can't protect you any longer. I want to believe that you can take care of yourself.

There are times when I don't know that you're upset or worried or frightened — you're beginning to learn to hide your feelings by keeping them inside and private. I'm afraid you think I wouldn't understand how you felt if you did share your feelings with me. Maybe it is a good idea to hide your feelings some of the time, but I know that if we do that too often, it can hurt us. I've been hurt sometimes by keeping my thoughts to myself too much because I was afraid, or I didn't know how to share them. I've also been hurt, and I have hurt others by sharing them too quickly or without thinking about how my actions might affect another person.

I remember a time when you thought I was the most important person in the world. You saw the world through my eyes. I guess it would be easier for me if you still did that. I do want to remain very important to you, but down deep inside, I want you to be able to listen to what others are saying and to be able to decide what value their ideas have. I can no longer make all decisions for you; I don't even want to. What I really want is for you to be able to make your own decisions but make them thoughtfully. I also need to be reassured that you can make good decisions, or I'm going to worry that you'll be hurt or will hurt someone else.

I keep asking myself if I taught you all the things I needed to teach you when you were younger. I get so frightened when I read or hear about other young people getting themselves into trouble — making such big mistakes that they could be affected by them for the rest of their lives. I know that I may, at times, ask more questions about what you say and do because of the foolish decisions people your age have made. I want you to realize that I am still responsible for many of the decisions which must be made involving your life. I accept that responsibility.

Don't be afraid to share your ideas and needs. Be wise enough to say "no" to others when you feel that they are wrong. Learn to make decisions based on long-range consequences and not just the immediate pleasure you may receive. Happiness is knowing and using the skills that allow you to be in control of your own life, and no one wants you to be happy more than I do.

I love you,

C

Birth Order Activity

Objective:

To help students become better acquainted with others in their group, especially those who are in the same birth placement in their families

Time:

One or two sessions

Procedures:

1. Advisor will divide advisees into groupings of birth order in family; i.e., oldest, youngest, middle, only.

2. Have students discuss positives and negatives they feel about their birth placement; i.e., being oldest allows me to _____
    and being oldest causes me frustrations because _____

3. Advisor should move from group to group to monitor discussion, throw out a question here and there, pass positive comments, etc.

4. Pull groups back together and have each give a brief summary.

5. Discuss these questions:

    Do students who are at different birth placement within a family have similar or dissimilar problems?

    Does it help you to understand your brothers/sisters better to hear of these concerns from your classmates?

ALTERNATIVE

Regroup students, mixing the birth orders to facilitate discussion about the differences experienced by each group.

C

Granny Hugs' Advice Column

Objective:

To help students identify common problems that relate to low self-esteem and to have a chance to offer advice and recommend solutions.

Time: Materials:

One or two sessions   "Granny Hugs" Handouts (4)

Procedures:

A mythical advice column is used as a format for exposing students to some ways to improve self-esteem. Say or paraphrase the following:

"Granny Hugs has an advice column for kids in a small town newspaper. As a result of raising a large family and being a good listener to her children, grandchildren, and their friends, she has developed an appreciation for how hard it is for kids to maintain high self-esteem. The following are some letters she has received and her responses. Let's read them and discuss what we agree or don't agree with. Then let's think about how we would answer the letters."

Dear Granny Hugs,

I feel like I'm worthless, like there is something wrong with me. I'll never be what people expect me to be so why bother trying? I'll never amount to anything.

A Failure

Dear Not a Failure,

You're a person who is good at some things and not so good at other things, just like everyone else. You can't always be the best or even do some things well and that's OK. Why remember and dwell on only your defeats? Many people are under a kind of negative self-hypnosis. They put labels on themselves. They say: I am (a) a terrible person who (b) always does awful things and (c) can't possibly do better. Instead of convincing yourself beforehand that something you want to do is impossible, why not spend your energy looking for ways to do it? Why not encourage yourself? You can't do anything if you believe you can't. But when you insist you're not the kind of person who can do something, all you are saying is that up to now you haven't done it. Who knows what you will do in the future? Anything is possible because you're changing all the time.

Create a mental picture of yourself as the kind of person you would like to be. Hold onto this picture tightly, never let it fade. The mind always tries to create in real life what it pictures. So always picture yourself as successful, no matter how badly things seem to be going at the moment. Then start doing little things that make you proud of yourself. Gradually you'll start doing bigger and harder things. You won't become super-confident overnight. It will take a while to break your old thinking style. But be patient. It can be done. Realize that even if you fail now and then, you are not a failure. You're simply learning!

Granny 6-ə

Is there anything you would add?

Dear Granny Hugs,

After I blow a test I always tell myself I'll do better next time because I'll study beforehand.
After I get my report card I promise my parents I'll try to raise my grades and really intend to
but it never seems to happen. I'd like to change but I can't get myself to.

A Failure

Dear Not a Failure,

Though it may sound strange, you have to like yourself and accept yourself before you can
change yourself. Liking yourself doesn't mean you have to think you're perfect or that
there's nothing about yourself you wish were different. It just means you accept yourself as
a person with both strengths and faults.

Let me give you an example of what I mean. Suppose you know someone who is really shy in
groups. She's a lot of fun with one or two people, but as soon as she gets into a crowd she
acts weird. If you don't like her just because she can't get along in a crowd and you put her
down for it, it's only going to make her feel more of a failure and she'll act more insecure.
But if you like her as she is and accept her as a human being and she knows that she's liked
and understood as she is, she has a good chance of improving.

Now, try to apply the same reasoning to yourself. If you don't like yourself and are always
putting yourself down because you don't study, it's going to be hard for you to believe that
you can make any changes or improvements. If you can accept that you're really okay as
you are, but you'd like to be a better "you," you have a chance. The next thing to do is to
talk yourself into taking steps each day. Do this by imagining how good you'll feel getting the
grades you want. Get a clear picture of it. Then visualize how bad you'd feel getting low
grades again. Tell yourself you've decided to study for just ten minutes. (Anyone can give
up watching TV or doing something else he/she wants to do for ten minutes.) At the end of
ten minutes picture yourself handing in your assignment the next day or doing well on a test
and how good it would feel. Then picture how you would feel if you didn't get it done or
didn't do well on the test. If you picture it clearly enough you'll find yourself wanting to
spend more than just ten minutes now that you have gotten started.

Granny

Is there anything you would add?

You answer this letter

Dear Granny Hugs,

Somewhere I got the idea that it's "bad" to like yourself. So when I do something I'm proud of and I start to feel good, I begin to criticize myself for liking myself too much. I know it's dumb, but I always do it. If people compliment me for something I've done, I feel if I don't say it wasn't really very good, they'll think I have a big head.

                                                  Embarrassed

Dear Embarrassed,

You answer this letter

Dear Granny Hugs,

I have a hard time raising my hand in class, even when I'm sure of the answer. I always think someone else can give a better answer, or that what I have to say isn't that important.

Invisible

Dear Invisible,

C

"Me" Collage

Objective:

To help students develop greater self-awareness

Time:

Two or more sessions

Materials:

Magazines, scissors, glue,
tag board, or construction paper

Procedures:

1. Students should cut out pictures, words and symbols that they feel are representative of themselves — things they like to do, things they own, things they would like to own, places they've been, people they admire, etc. Magazines should be collected well in advance. The art department, home economics department and library sometimes have extra magazines. Parents can help as well by contributing magazines.

2. Then they are to paste these pictures, words and symbols onto a paper to make a collage. The shape of their collages is completely up to the individual.

3. After the collages are finished, display them in the classroom.

4. Have each student explain to the class some of the items in his/her collage.

5. You might have them work their own name into the arrangement of the collage.

C

Personal Coat of Arms

Objective:

To help students understand the full meaning of the word *value*

Time: **Materials:**

One or two sessions   "Personal Coal of Arms" handout

Procedures:

1. Say to the students: The most important step in self-understanding is being able to clarify or state what you value. Once you know what you value you can set goals and objectives and make personal decisions which will be satisfying to you. You will be asked to do some activities today which will help you identify or discover what your values are.

   Many times a person does not recognize adequately just what he or she values. It takes some thought and examination of behavior to know this. Values change as someone grows older. You would recognize this if you had been asked to list three things you valued as fifth graders and compared them with your list today. Values change with age because a person or a group may influence you to change. For example, students may choose to change a value from getting good grades to pleasing their friends.

   Sometimes a person senses a conflict of values. This often causes a dilemma because the choice you must make may mean you cannot satisfy two values that conflict with each other. An example of this would be giving test answers to your friend (cheating *vs* value of honesty) and loyalty to your friend (friendship *vs* dishonesty). Think of a values conflict that you have faced.

2. Share with the group an example from your own (teacher's) life of a time when you felt anxiety, stress, or conflict because you were forced to choose between conflicting values.

3. Ask the students how they felt when they were forced to choose between conflicting values.

4. Distribute "Personal Coat of Arms" and have students complete it.

DIRECTIONS: Select the coat of arms shaped like an African war shield or the shield derived from European heraldry. Enlarge and reproduce the shield on butcher or other paper or half a poster board.

Create an individual coat of arms by drawing in the appropriate section words or sketches that express your thoughts regarding each of the following:

1. The most significant event in your life from birth to age ten.
2. The most significant event in your life from age ten to present.
3. Your greatest success or achievement in the past year.
4. Your happiest moment in the past year.
5. What you would attempt to do if you had one year to live and were guaranteed success in whatever you attempted.
6. Something you are good at.
7. Three words you would most like to be said of you if you died today (place at the bottom of the shield).

Some optional questions could be substituted for those listed above:

1. What is something you are striving to become or be?
2. What is your family's greatest achievement?
3. Name two things you do well.
4. Name the three people who have been most influential in your life.

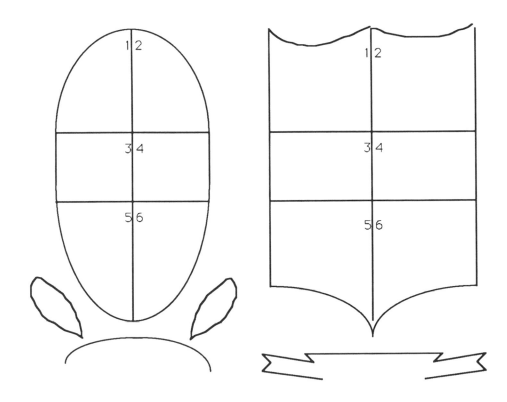

Promises, Promises

Objective:

To understand the feelings involved when promises are made and the feelings involved when promises are kept or broken.

Time:

One session plus a follow-up

Procedures:

Arrange seats in circle.

Begin by discussion these questions:

1. What is a promise?

2. What is a favor?

3. How does it feel to have a friend break a promise?

4. How does it feel to break a promise?

5. How do you feel when you ask a favor and are rejected?

6. What are white lies? Are they OK?

Ask for a volunteer in the group who would like to request a favor from someone in the group. Then ask someone to promise to fulfill the favor. KEEP A WRITTEN RECORD OF REQUESTS AND PROMISES.

Allow all student volunteers to make favor requests and get promises from others to fulfill their requests.

Although all students should be encouraged to participate, no one should be forced to ask a favor or make a promise.

FOLLOW-UP: At a later time, check up on the promises made to see if they were kept.

c

Experiencing Trust

Objectives:
To help students identify conditions that encourage trust and .
to assist them in identifying different levels of trust.

Time:
One session

Materials:
See below

Procedures:

Each student should be given a copy of the following list or copy it from the board:

1. Imitate the crowing of a rooster.

2. Give a two-minute talk about your best qualities.

3. Do a silent pantomime of a very sleepy person brushing his teeth.

4. Give a two-minute talk on what you like most about your classmates.

5. Recite a short nursery rhyme you remember from your childhood.

6. Balance a book on your head and walk across the room.

7. Read a short passage of your choice from a book that is available in the room.

Ask each student to number the activities on his/her list from one to seven, in the order of what he would most prefer doing in front of the group to what he would least prefer doing. Explain how individuals may be called upon to actually perform one of their first three choices, so they should give serious thought to their choices. When everyone has completed the list, ask by a show of hands how many put "imitate a rooster" first, and how many put it last. Do the same with each item, recording the results. When you have the numbers recorded, go through the list again, asking someone who put the item as his first choice to actually perform the activity. Skip any item not chosen for a first choice to avoid embarrassing anyone. After the performances are over (these need not take long since they have no value in themselves but merely serve to keep the exercise "honest"), you can initiate discussion. Review the statistics about which activities were chosen first and last and ask the students to comment why they think certain items were rated the way they were.   (continued)

From this point you will want to get into the main concern of the topic by using some of the following questions:

1. Did you feel uneasy about performing one of the items on the list?

2. Do you think everyone listed the items in the order of the least to the most embarrassing to do in front of a group? Is this a usual reaction?

3. In what way do you think the ordering of the list is an indication of our ability to trust others? Is it also a measure of how we trust ourselves? Why?

4. Which is safer to do, something silly in a group like an imitation of a rooster, or something serious, like talk about your own good qualities? Why?

5. Is our ability to trust others and our ability to trust ourselves two aspects of the same thing?

6. What would happen in a group like this is no one was able to trust others except in superficial things like imitating a rooster? Are there situations you've been in where matters never get beyond the level of silliness? What is it like? What do you think is the reason for it? What would it take to overcome this kind of situation?

D

Success Experience Activity

Objective:
To help students focus on their success experiences.

Time:
One session

Materials:
Worksheet "Success Experiences Activity"

Procedures:

1. List twelve specific achievements or successful experiences. Ask class for examples to start off.

2. Distribute the worksheet and say to the students: "Place a check in each box which explains why this was an achievement for you. Do this for each of your achievements."

3. "Read each one of your success experiences, review each of the checked statements — which was the most important one in making you feel successful? Place this letter in the last column. Do this for each of your success experiences."

4. "Which letter appears most frequently? Write the statement on the first line of the box."

5. "Write the total of each vertical column at the bottom."

6. "Identify the highest total and write that statement on the second line."
   (If you have already used that statement, go to the next highest.)

7. "Combine these two statements and write your own definition of success."

8. OPTIONAL: Have small groups make a 24 square inch symbol of what success means.

INPUT

Achievements	A I used skill and know-how	B I was free to decide what I did or how I did it	C I influenced somebody — got him/her to do what I wanted	D I met a challenge or had an adventure	E I helped someone else do something important to him/her
1					
2					
3					
4					
5					
6					
7					
8					
9					
10					
11					
12					
COLUMN TOTALS					

OUTPUT

F I increased my self-respect	G I received recognition, support or respect from others	H I received money or its equivalent	I I received love and acceptance from my family	J I learned something new

As Others See Us

Objective:

To reveal the positive feelings advisory classmates have for one another

Time:

One or two session

Materials:

Butcher paper for tracing hand or foot, pen/pencil

Procedures:

1. Divide students into pairs

2. Each student draws an outline of his/her partner's hand or foot. Put name on paper and leave on desk.

3. Each student moves around the room (and passes "hands") stopping to write one positive comment on each hand or foot that he/she feels describes that person.

4. Break into groups of four for discussion or, if not too large, keep as one large group. How do students feel about the comments? Do they think they are accurate? Did they learn something new about themselves?

5. Students are allowed to take home the descriptions of themselves or, if they choose, fashion them into a collage for the room. (Individual hands should be mounted on a piece of paper if taken home)

Student of the Week

Objectives:
To recognize that each student has unique qualities and to encourage students to be positive with one another.

Time:
One session

Materials:
Posterboard, magic markers, construction paper, crayons, glue

Procedures:
Stress the fact that each student has many good qualities and encourage the students to be very positive and honest in writing down other people's strong points. Assure students that they will all have a turn.

1. Decide on a way of choosing a "Student of the Week," for example, draw names out of a hat, or pick a number and have students guess to see who can come closest to your number.

2. Write the student's name in large letters at the top of the poster and/or put a picture of that student on the poster.

3. Choose a symbol such as a circle, square, triangle, etc; then cut these patterns out of construction paper and pass one out to each student.

4. Ask each student to think of at least one nice thing to write about the "Student of the Week." It must be positive. It might be something about physical appearance or a special quality or ability that this person possesses; or it might be a reason why the student likes this particular person.

5. Have each student glue his pattern to the poster. An artistic student may organize these pieces in a design. Display the poster in the classroom, team area, or in a hallway.

6. Give the selected student something special, such as a cupcake or a little gift. The student of the week may also be called upon to be the message person, class host, or to assume other special responsibility for the week.

7. Encourage everyone to make "The Student" feel special that week. Inform the administration of the student selected so recognition from that quarter can be received.

VARIATION:
Instead of writing positive statements about the student, have students use magazines to cut out descriptive adjectives which apply to the "Student of the Week" and glue them onto the poster. For example: honest, friendly, pretty, etc. Short rhyming verses are another option.

E

Get the Message

Objective:
To help students identify and understand the interaction of the four communication process components.

Time:
Two sessions

Materials:
Worksheet: "The Communication Process"

Procedures:

1. Put vocabulary words on the board:

    sender: person giving or sending message
    receiver: person for whom the message is intended
    message: information you wish to get across
    feedback: reaction from the receiver that shows he/she got the message

2. Draw a diagram of the communication process on the chalkboard or overhead transparency. Use a number of different examples from the school, home, social life of a student to indicate components of the process. Gradually ask student to supply examples, as well.

3. Have students diagram the communication process in the worksheet you distribute. Assign parts of worksheet to different students or have all do all examples.

4. Discuss results:
    — What can happen if your verbal and your nonverbal messages conflict?
    — How important is it that you get feedback from others when you are communicating with them?
    — When there is a communication problem, can you tell if the problem is located in the message, the sender, the receiver, or feedback element? Try some examples.

PERSONAL APPLICATION
    — When do you need to communicate at school? When are you the sender?
    — How are you at sending verbal messages? Are they clear? audible?
    — How are you at sending nonverbal messages? Do they always agree with what you have said?
    — How do you usually give feedback, verbally or nonverbally?

THE COMMUNICATION PROCESS

<u>The teacher</u> → <u>"Jack, please come here."</u> → <u>Jack</u>
sender   *message*   *receiver*

↖   <u>Jack nods, and starts toward teacher,</u>   ↙
feedback

For the five examples below draw a diagram of the communication process that indicates who is the sender, who is the receiver, what is the message (verbal and nonverbal) and what is the feedback, if any. Draw a diagram for each of the examples.

1. Mary says to Ann, "I really hate that new guy, Troy. He's a creep." She looks adoringly at Troy. Ann says, "Sure."

2. The teacher asks, "What's the matter, Nick?" Nick slouches, looks at the floor and says, "Nothing."

3. Mr. Brown says, "Who's helping with the dishes tonight?" Mrs. Brown looks at him and throws him the dishtowel.

4. Paul tells his friend Jack, "Meet me at 3:30 at the track." His friend says, "OK, three-thirty on the dot."

5. The teacher announces, "Friday there will be a field trip to the zoo." The class's thirty faces smile.

E

Thumbs Down on Roadblocks

Objective:
To help students will understand four roadblocks to communication.

Time:
Two sessions

Materials:
Worksheets: "Communication Roadblocks" and "Who Said That"

Procedures:

1. Introduce the activity by stating the concept of roadblocks to communication. Share the definition of roadblocks as people's behaviors that get in the way of good communication..

2. Distribute worksheet "Communication Roadblocks". Explain how certain behaviors of the sender can get in the way of the communication process. Ask students to look at the descriptive words on the worksheet. For each set of words, think of an example of a person using these approaches to communicate a message. As examples are brainstormed, discuss the *consequences* of a communication using each approach. Ask students to explain why this approach is a roadblock.

    Explain that the roadblocks can be grouped into four types of communicators. Demonstrate each type, asking students to identify which roadblocks they are using. Discuss: What body posture, gestures go with each type? Have you ever had to deal with any of these roadblocks?

    Assign four students the task of role playing the planning of a class party. Secretly assign each student a different roadblock role. Allow five minutes for them to plan skit. Have group present skit, class guess who is playing which role.

3. Hand out worksheet "Who Said That." Ask students to match the person in the drawing to the appropriate roadblock statement, and label the drawings appropriately.

PERSONAL APPLICATION
Discuss: Which of the roadblock people are you most like? least like?
What's the best way to handle people who use roadblocks?

 COMMUNICATION ROADBLOCKS

Listed below on the left hand side are some roadblocks to communication. When people use these behaviors, they often prevent communication from taking place.

Read each set of descriptive words and think of an example of how someone has acted this way to prevent communication.

DESCRIPTION OF BEHAVIOR	EXAMPLE

BLAMER

1. Orders, directs, commands

   You said: "I'd like to do ..."

2. Warns, threatens

   The Blamer responded:

3. Moralizes, preaches

4. Judges, criticizes, blames

5. Name-calls, ridicules, shames

PLEASER

6. Obliges

   You said: "I think I ..."

7. Praises, agrees, approves

   The Pleaser responded:

8. Reassures, sympathizes, consoles

COMPUTER

9. Advises, gives solutions

   You said: "I'm really interested in ..."

10. Lectures, persuades logically

    The Computer responded:

11. Probes, interrogates

DISTRACTOR

12. Withdraws, distracts

    You said: "I'm planning to ..."

13. Humors, diverts

    The Distractor responded:

WHO SAID THAT?

Label each roadblock person, 1, 2, 3, and 4. Roadblock person labels are Blamer, Pleaser, Computer, Distractor. Label each of the following statements with the number of the *roadblock person* you think must have said it.

1.

2.

STATEMENTS

a. It's 11:40 and 20 seconds___

b. You are really an idiot. ___

c. Anything you say is OK. ___

d. My idea is, oops, I fell. ___

e. We can't get anything done with you in the group. ___

f. Refreshments are necessary at a dance.___

g. How about some nice, hot, tea?___

h. The main thing we need to do is, omigosh, a bee! ____

3.

4.

The Big 6 Communication Skills

Objective:
To help students identify and demonstrate the six positive communication skills.

Time:
Two to three sessions

Materials:
Two worksheets

Procedures:

Introduce activity by reviewing the concept of verbal and nonverbal communication.

Discuss: When someone is talking to you, how do you indicate that you are receiving the message? Define: active listening.

Did you know that you can actually help communicate better by using active listening skills?
1. Give students a model situation by role-playing. Your best friend comes up to you and says, "My mother always blames me for everything that happens."
2. Ask: How would you respond? What would you do or say?
3. Make up situations that apply to your school, social activities typical family interactions.

Review the "Big 6 Communication Skills" using the handouts.
1. Demonstrate how a teacher could use each of the six skills in response to a student's comment, "I couldn't find my homework."

2. Demonstrate some of the body language skills that can be used with active listening, e.g., eye contact, smile, nod, posture. Ask students to "read" what message is conveyed.

3. Break students into groups and assign each one of the Big 6 skills to demonstrate in a situation. Allow five minutes to practice; circulate through the groups to monitor, suggest, and provide feedback.

4. Have each group present its situation; the audience members must identify which of the Big 6 skills is being demonstrated.

THE BIG 6 COMMUNICATION SKILLS

Here are some skills you can use to help the communication process. They are called the Big 6 active listening skills. They are called active listening because they require you, the listener, to say or do certain things to help make sure the "message" gets across. Active listening helps the person who is talking feel comfortable talking to you.

SKILL	DESCRIPTION	EXAMPLE
1. Ask questions	**Find out more** about what the person says, ask for more information: who? how? why?	Friend: "I *hate* science!" Ask "Why do you say that?"
2. Be supportive	**Show you care about what the person is saying,** be sympathetic towards him/her and what	Teacher: "I have so many papers to correct tonight!" Active listener: "You work too hard."
3. Clarify	**Make sure you get the message clearly.** Do you mean... I understand, except for ...	Friend: "I'd really like to go with you but I can't." Active listener: "You mean your mom won't let you go shopping?"
4. Reflect	Show the other person that **you are aware** of what he/she is saying. You sound like... You seem... Are you saying...	Mother: "There's a lot to be done if we want supper on time tonight! Active listener: "Sounds as if you could use some help."
5. Avoid argument	Arguing prevents good communication. **Rather than arguing,** say "um hm," "oh," or remain silent... let the person say whât he/she wants to say.	Friend: "I think that math work is too hard." Active listener: "Oh..."
6. Avoid giving unsolicited	**Don't give advice,** unless it's asked for. It's better to ask the other person what he/she wants to do, feels, thinks.	Friend: "What should I wear? Active listener: "What do you think looks good?"

THE BIG 6 COMMUNICATIONS SKILLS

MORE PRACTICE

Write an active listening response for each of these situations. Label the responses A through F to show which response you used. Write the response in the speech balloon for the active listener.

A. Friend: *I'd really like to go to the game tonight.*

Response ___

B. Fellow student: *The history test was unfair. It was supposed to be all multiple choice questions, not essay answers.*

Response ___

C. Mom: *Kids today don't realize how good they have it.*

Response ___

D. Teacher: *I'm disappointed in the way you've been behaving lately in class.*

Response ___

E. Friend: *You know, sometimes you act really dumb.*

Response ___

F. Friend: *What do you think I should do about the kid who's bugging me?*

Response ___

E

Communication Stoppers

Objective:

To assist students in improving their verbal communication by studying seven "communication stoppers."

Time:

One session

Materials:

Chalk, chalkboard, seven scripts
for student role-playing

Procedures:

1. Discuss with students the factors they think block good verbal communication. List on board.

2. Divide 14 of the students into pairs and give them a role-playing script to practice. Give them a few minutes to get comfortable with the scripts.

3. Ask first pair of students to read the script out loud with "feeling." Following the script, ask class to identify the communication "stopper."

4. Complete all seven scripts listing all the "stoppers" on the board. Discuss with class, emphasizing "stoppers" and clarifying student perceptions.

5. Ask each student to write the definition of each "stopper" and write a script to illustrate the "stopper." Each need not be long but must illustrate what is happening. This can be an assignment done outside of class. As time permits review and raise questions.

COMMUNICATION STOPPERS

1. **Interrupting**

   Person 1:   Guess what? I learned to divide fractions today.

   Person 2:   I learned that last week. The thing that is really hard is formulas.

   Person 1:   Oh, really? I was so happy when I finally learned how to …

   Person 2:   Formulas are very hard; interesting, though. Once you understand the formula you are working on, it's fun. The most interesting formula for me is the way you find out the diameter of a circle.

   Person 1:   Oh. I haven't gotten to formulas yet. When I learned to multiply fractions I felt the same way. I …

   Person 2:   Multiplying fractions is easy. I can teach you how.

   Person 1:   I already know how. What was hard for me was

                understanding how to divide them I just …

   Person 2:   My big sister is taking trigonometry. If you think fractions are complicated, you should see her trigonometry book. There are more numbers and little symbols in there! It really looks hard.

   Person 1:   I guess trigonometry is just as hard for her as fractions are for us. My cousin …

   Person 2:   Naw. Trigonometry isn't hard for her. She enjoys it. I'll tell her to help you with your fractions. She can teach you how to multiply and divide them.

   Person 1:   But … I already know.

   Person 2:   Hey! I have to go now … see you later …

2. **Probing**

   Person 1:   Hi! Say …I wanted to tell you that I went to my grandparents' farm last weekend and …

   Person 2:   Which grandparents?

   Person 1:   My mother's parents. Anyway, I was at the farm and I …

   Person 2:   Where is their farm?

   Person 1:   It's about 30 miles north of here.

   Person 2:   Up in the mountains?

   Person 1:   No, close to the mountains, but not up in the mountains. Anyway, when I was at their farm, I learned how to milk their cow, and …

   Person 2:   Who taught you?

   Person 1:   My mother.

   Person 2:   Your mother? I thought you were at your grandparents' farm.

Person 1:	Yes, but my mother grew up there and she knows how to milk cows.
Person 2:	Oh. Did it take you long to learn?
Person 1:	No ... Anyway ... I
Person 2:	Why did you want to milk the cow?
Person 1:	Because I ...because I did, I just did.
Person 2:	Did you drink any of the milk?
Person 1:	No.
Person 2:	Well, why not?
Person 1:	No.
Person 2:	Well, why not?
Person 1:	That's what I've been trying to tell you. The cow stepped right into the bucket of milk.
Person 2:	Well, why did the cow to that?
Person 1:	I don't know. Why don't you ask the COW!

3. Interpreting

Person 1:	What did you do last weekend?
Person 2:	I stayed home and read a book.
Person 1:	Oh. You're on restriction again.
Person 2:	No. I just felt like doing it.
Person 1:	You must be behind in your school work again.
Person 2:	No. I am all caught up.
Person 1:	Aw, come on. The teacher made you do it.
Person 2:	No. It wasn't because of the teacher.
Person 1:	Then you're just trying to get in good with the teacher.
Person 2:	The teacher doesn't even know about it.
Person 1:	It must have been a pretty boring weekend.
Person 2:	No. I really enjoyed it.
Person 1:	You're WEIRD!

4. Confronting

Person 1:	I hit a home run!
Person 2:	Well, do you have to brag about it?
Person 1:	Well, I do feel good about it.
Person 2:	You brag all the time. It's hard to listen to.

Person 1:	Oh. Does it bother you?
Person 2:	Yeah, and that's not all. You make me nervous the way you play. You're always trying to steal a base and taking chances. I wish you'd cut it out!
Person 1:	Well, so far so good. I don't make an out very often.
Person 2:	That's just because you're lucky. You drive me crazy the way you play.
Person 1:	Gee. That's too bad. I only do my best.
Person 2:	Well, your best ain't much. You just don't concentrate like you should.
Person 1:	Oh. Say, how have you been doing lately?
Person 2:	Forget about me. You are the one with the problem!

5. Advising

Person 1:	Hey. What's the matter?
Person 2:	Oh, I've got a problem.
Person 1:	What is it?
Person 2:	One of my friends is moving away.
Person 1:	Oh. Don't get upset about it. Just make some new friends.
Person 2:	Well, I probably will. It's just that I'm really going to miss my friend.
Person 1:	Don't feel so sorry for yourself. Friends come and go. You'll get over it. Take my advice and just go make some new friends.
Person 2:	Well, that's easy for you to say; it's not your friend.
Person 1:	It's happened to me before. I just forget about it. That's what you ought to do.

6. Dominating

Person 1:	Hi. I wanted to tell you about what I did last night.
Person 2:	Oh. What was it?
Person 1:	I went to the football game with my aunt and uncle and we ...
Person 2:	I went to the game last weekend. I went with one friend and then we saw some of my other friends there. We sat together and cheered for the team. We cheered louder than anybody there. All the people around us were cheering too.
Person 1:	I cheered too, but the team lost the game. They almost won, but ...
Person 2:	Yeah, I heard 'bout it. In the last few minutes the other team made another touchdown. Reminds me of all those games last year. We lost so many close games in the last few minutes that we should have won.

| Person 1: | Even if we lost, it was still a good game. Y… |
| Person 2: | Yeah, but not as good as the one I saw. Last week the team was really playing well. We started off with two touchdowns in the first quarter. The best play was made when they intercepted thatpass and ran it back for a touchdown. Wow! Everybody just went wild. |

| Person 1: | I know. We intercepted two passes last night, but … |
| Person 2: | Best game I ever saw. I liked the way it ended too. They just held those guys back for the entire last quarter. Those guys just couldn't move the ball at all because our defense was so good. They kept calling for time out and trying different plays, but nothing worked. Well, I have to go now. Thanks for telling me about last night's game. See yah! |

7. Putting down

| Person 1: | Say, you knothead, watch where you're going! |
| Person 2: | Oh, did I step on your foot? |

| Person 1: | What's the matter with you? Are you weird or something? Couldn't you feel it? |
| Person 2: | Gee, no. I didn't. I'm sorry. |

| Person 1: | Well, get with it, stupid. |
| Person 2: | Listen! I said I was sorry! |

| Person 1: | Yeah, yeah. You're sorry and that makes if OK. You're a real dummy. |
| Person 2: | Look, you jerk. If you don't want to get stepped on, stay out of the way! |

| Person 1: | Who do you think you are calling a jerk, you big dope. |
| Person 2: | You … you big idiot. |

| Person 1: | I'm no idiot! |
| Person 2: | You sure are … you bonehead idiot! |

| Person 1: | I'm not!! |
| Person 2: | Yes, you are. |

| Person 1: | Dingbat! |
| Person 2: | Weirdo! |

| Person 1: | Creep! |
| Person 2: | … |

Agree To Disagree

Objective:
To assist students in learning how to disagree without being disagreeable.

Time:
One session

Materials:
Worksheet

Procedures:

1. Teacher reads or paraphrases the paragraphs below:

There are times when people disagree with each other. They disagree in different ways. Some get angry. Roy thinks everyone should think the way he does. He doesn't want to hear another point of view. He doesn't listen to other people. He calls them "silly" or "crazy." He thinks yelling at them will make them change their minds. It only makes them dislike him.

Then there are those who listen. Leroy states his opinion, but he lets others talk, too. He knows there are two sides to a question. He doesn't get angry, and his friends enjoy talking with him. They like him even if he does disagree with them.

Keep these rules in mind when discussing a subject with someone.

   a. Be clear in your thinking *so you can communicate* your point of view effectively.

   b. Listen *as well as talk so* you can understand the other person's point of view.

   c. *Stay calm.* Don't lose your temper. If you do, you can't have a good discussion. The other person might get angry, too. You could lose the argument, even a friend.

2. Hand out worksheets for students to complete individually or in groups that will act out the situations.

3. Go over correct responses, the ones which are not impolite. Have students write in other appropriate responses.

4. Students might like to think up good responses to additional statements like, "That skating party sounds like fun."

5. Generate a list of reasons for forming neutral responses.

Agree to Disagree

Can you disagree in such a way that you are still a likable person? Here is a test you can take. Pretend you are listening to a number of discussions. You are going to decide which response is best in each case. Put an X on the line beside the answer you choose.

A. Statement: **I think school should have short summer vacations.**
   Responses: _____ You're crazy!
   _____ I don't think they're long enough now.
   _____ You always say stupid things.

   _____
   (write in)

B. Statement: **We ought to play football every day for recess.**
   Responses: _____ I hate football.
   _____ I love basketball.
   _____ That might get boring.

   _____
   (write in)

C. Statement: **Our basketball team lost again.**
   Responses _____ They tried.
   _____ They're all wimps anyway.
   _____ Tell somebody who cares.

   _____
   (write in)

D. Statement: **Mr. Jones is a great teacher.**
   Responses: _____ That's your opinion.
   _____ He's a very sloppy dresser.
   _____ My sister received a bad progress report from him.

   _____
   (write in)

E. Statement: **I think it is going to rain.**
   Responses: _____ You're no weatherman.
   _____ I don't see any clouds.
   _____ You're never right about anything.

   _____
   (write in)

F. Statement: **This weekend, I'm going fishing.**
   Responses: _____ What a waste of time.
   _____ I'd rather read a book.
   _____ You're too stupid to catch anything.

   _____
   (write in)

Rumors

Objectives:
To experience how easily rumors get started.
To evaluate statements for fact, opinion, and misinterpretation.
To create alternatives to spreading rumors.

Time:
Three sessions probably needed

Procedures:

1.   At the close of a previous session, introduce this activity which involves problems resulting from rumors by sharing the following nursery rhyme with the class:

> Jack and Jill went up the hill
> to fetch a pail of water
> Jack fell down and
> broke his crown
> And Jill came tumbling after

2.   At the next session start by saying such things as:

"Did you see Jack's face? I heard that he and Jill had a fight on the hill," said Tweedle-Dum. "Gosh! I didn't know Jill was so rough," said Tweedle-Dee. "Maybe she hit him with the bucket," replied Tweedle-Dum. "Hey! What were they doing up on the hill anyway?" wondered Tweedle-Dee.

3.   Put on board this definition from Webster's Student Dictionary:

> rumor (roo'mer), n. 1. A popular report; common talk. 2. A story that gets about without anyone's knowing how it started. -v.t. To tell or spread rumor.

4.   Point out that many hurt and angry feelings result from gossip and rumors. Rumors have a snowball effect and quickly get out of control. Explain that the following activities will help them handle themselves better in these situations and become more aware of consequences and alternatives. Most examples used really have happened!

5.   Introduce the TELEPHONE GAME or BUZZ BUZZ with necessary ground rules.

   The teacher whispers one of the five examples below to a student. The student then passes it on word for word to another and that student passes it on to another and so on. The last student announces out loud to the class what he has heard. The teacher reads the original statement for comparison.

E

    a. Wouldn't it be funny if Jack and Jill were going together?

    b. Jill makes me so mad when she does that! I could just hit her!

    c. Hey, we don't have to study so hard because it will be an open book test. My head hurts anyway.

    d. I hope we have a Valentine's Day dance so I might get a chance to dance with Jack.

    e. Jill looks like a cow when she wears that dress.

6. Alternative procedures:

    a. Instead of passing it on word for word, the student prefaces it with "I heard him (or her) say that…"

    b. The class is divided in half and each group whispers the same message to see which group is more accurate.

7. Wrap up by discussing such questions as the following:

    a. How accurately was the example passed along?

    b. How would you feel if you made the original statement?

    c. How would you feel if you were Jack or Jill and heard your name mentioned?

8. Probably at a second session, introduce the topic of building and squelching rumors. Have students look at the 5 examples in the BUZZ - BUZZ activity. Teacher may generate other examples and decide which parts of each are **fact** or **opinion**. (Which words signal **opinions**? Underline them.)

    FACT
    OPINION - FACT
    FACT (first part), OPINION (might)
    OPINION (looks like - it seems to me)

9. Discuss how might each example be misinterpreted and/or on its way to becoming a rumor?

    a. I'm going to hit Jill.
       When I'm mad, I hit.

    b. We don't have to study.
       We're not having a test.
       Studying hurts my head.

    c. We're having a Valentine's Day dance.
       I'm going with Jack.

    d. Jill is a cow.
       Jill is ugly.
       I don't like Jill's clothes.

10. Lead students in generating some squelching statements that might stop or prevent misinterpretation.

"Don't believe everything you hear."

"That's not true. They're probably just jealous."

11. To provide practice in brainstorming and evaluating alternatives divide the class into small groups or do as a teacher-directed activity with the entire class.

12. Ask students to *brainstorm* the following questions. Think of as many possible reasons as you can. It doesn't matter if it's a good reason or a bad reason.

   a. Why do people spread rumors? To make others mad; to hurt people's feelings; it's interesting; they're just kidding around; for attention; to look "big."

   b. How can you help stop a rumor? Don't participate; don't say anything; don't listen to it — ignore it; squelch it ("How do you know it's true? "That's mean!" "You shouldn't say things like that.")

13. Divide the class into small groups. Have each group work on one of the problems below utilizing brainstorming to generate many solutions (good, bad, indifferent) and then evaluate the solutions, choosing one or two that would be in keeping with school rules and in minimizing hurt feelings.

   (Alternative Procedure: Have each group *role-play* the situation and solution and discuss how each participant felt.)

   a. Your best friend has told you that he heard other students talking about you and one is planning to beat you up. You tell a few more of your friends and before you know it, a big fight is planned.

   b. You arrive at school and a group of your friends ignore you and walk away. Later, one of them angrily tells you that you shouldn't have been talking about her family and calling her names. (You never did talk about them.)

   c. You are taking aspirin at the water fountain. Two boys jokingly announce to a nearby teacher that you're on drugs, that you're "popping pills." Other students hear too. Later that day the counselor calls you in to investigate possible drug abuse.

   d. You are new to the school. You hear some students that you have just been getting to know talking about others and calling them some ugly names. They ask for your agreement. You want to be their friend but don't like what they're saying.

   e. You are friendly and like to help people. Your girlfriend has heard from other girls that you are "messing with them." This is not true, but your girlfriend won't believe you.

E

Putting It All Together

Objective:
To give students opportunities to demonstrate their knowledge of communication skills by applying them in role-played, simulated situations.

Time:
Three sessions

Materials:
Worksheets, "Interpersonal Relationships Evaluation"

Procedures:

FIRST SESSION:

Introduce activity by reviewing the concept of verbal and non-verbal communication. Review appropriate vocabulary. (Use spelling bee or quiz game format for interest.)

1. Divide students into groups of about five each. Hand each of the groups the Communication Worksheet which has a number of role-playing situation suggestions on it. Ask them to prepare a skit based on an assigned (or selected) numbered situation. Allow several minutes for the preparation of the skit.

2. Allow groups to present skits. Have "audience" identify specific features of interpersonal communication that were shown: verbal and non-verbal elements, message, sender, receiver, feedback, roadblocks, if any, etc.

3. Cut up message slips and distribute to class. Have students work in pairs to present the idea on a message slip to the class. The "audience" must guess which message is being sent. They may use "Guessing the Message," section on worksheet.

SECOND SESSION:

Distribute evaluation sheets. Have students complete them. Discuss what has happened in this unit on communication, asking students to share their ideas about the activities, how it helped them in school, what they liked, didn't like about particular activities.

THIRD SESSION:

Evaluation: Interpersonal Relationships Evaluation Questionnaire; Role-Play Performances; Completed IMPs and informal comments.

Communication Worksheet

I. **Vocabulary review** — can you define or give an example of each word?

interpersonal	communication	receiver
friendly behavior	verbal	feedback
characteristics	non-verbal	active listening
relationships	sender	roadblocks

II. **Role-play situations** — pick one of these situations and make up a skit that shows communication taking or not taking place.

1. Let the teacher know you don't understand.

2. Let a classmate know you would like to be friends.

3. Let someone know you are angry with him/her.

4. Help someone you don't know in an unfamiliar place, e.g., store, bus.

5. Show others you don't like the way they are behaving.

6. Show that you don't want to be disturbed.

7. Show that you are confident, comfortable in front of a group.

8. Say no to something your friends are trying to get you to do.

9. Show that you are pleased and happy with something.

10. Get people quiet.

11. Ask a parent an important question or favor.

12. Explain something to a teacher.

III. **Guessing the message.** Which of these messages is being role-played?

I'm glad to meet you.	I'm nervous.	I'd like to meet you.
I'm so excited.	My ... hurts.	I'm tired.
I'm bored.	I'm proud of my work.	I'm not interested.
I'm worried.	I'm impatient.	I can't see well.
I don't understand.	I feel terrific today.	I need help.
Ouch! That's hot.	I'm really interested.	I disapprove of what
I'm so confused, lost!	You're late.	you are doing.

MESSAGE SLIPS

Cut at dotted lines and give to students.

I'm glad to meet you.	I'm tired.
I'm so excited.	I'm so angry with you for being late.
I'm bored.	I'm impatient.
I'm worried.	I'm in love.
I'm nervous.	I'm not interested.
eye tooth My foot hurts ear	I can't see well
I'm proud of my work.	I have a question or I don't understand.
I'd like to meet you	I need help.
Ouch, That's hot.	I'm so confused, lost.
I feel terrific today!	I'm really interested!

Interpersonal Relationships Evaluation

DIRECTIONS: Pick the best answers for problems 1-4. Circle your choices.

1. The best definition for good communication is

   a. sending a message to another person.
   b. telling another person a message.
   c. getting a message across to another person so that it is understood as you meant it to be.
   d. speaking to another person every day.

2. Pick the way or ways that people communicate with each other.

   a. write a letter.
   b. talk to a friend.
   c. motion to someone to approach you.
   d. wink at your best friend.
   e. all of the above.

3. Communication has four basic parts or elements. They are

   a. sender, receiver, message, feedback.
   b. radio, receiver, message, frequency.
   c. people, message, words, meaning.
   d. radio, television, telephone, telegraph.
   e. none of the above.

4. "Feedback" is a word used when we talk about communication. Pick the best definition for feedback.

   a. give information to someone else.
   b. reaction from the receiver that shows he/she got the message.
   c. provide "feed" or food to someone.
   d. the communication process.
   e. all of the above.

5. Circle three non-verbal ways of communication in the list below:

   a. adult in police uniform.
   b. whisper.
   c. sing a song.
   d. wink.
   e. telephone message.
   f. frown.

6. You have lived on your street for five years and have been friends with several boys and girls there during that time. A new house built recently was sold to a family having two children — one in the fifth grade and one in the seventh grade. Both of the children seem to be shy and have not played with you or your friends since moving in about three weeks ago. So far, you have said "Hi" to them and they have answered "Hi" back to you. List three verbal behaviors and three nonverbal behaviors that you could use to make them feel more comfortable about getting to know you.

                Verbal   Nonverbal

7. Circle the letter in front of the four skills that open and maintain effective communication with others.

   a. ask questions.
   b. yell at others when you think they are wrong.
   c. give advice and criticism.
   d. avoid argument.
   e. use friendly body language.
   f. reflect meanings.
   g. lean away from others when talking.

8. Some people cut off communication by blaming others. List three verbal and three nonverbal behaviors of a blamer.

                Verbal   Nonverbal

9. The four common types of roadblockers are the blamer, the computer, the pleaser, and the distractor. Identify which type of roadblocker would make the statements given below.

   a. "It is 692.3 miles from our house to the beach."

   b. "You are a dumb somebody."

   c. "Gee, you're always right."

   d. "I want to go to the — hey, there's a hair on your shoulder."

   e. "We need 22 3/4 sandwiches for the party."

   f. "You should have known that you couldn't do that job."

10. Making and keeping friends require certain behaviors. List three behaviors that you find helpful in making and keeping friends. Then, list three behaviors that are not helpful in making and keeping friends.

Helpful   Not helpful

11. A classmate gives you a piece of cake from his/her lunch. You like this friendly behavior and wish to show your feelings. What can you say and do to show how you feel? List your responses below.

12. Label each part of the communication process and fill in the correct information.

_____ ⇨ _____ ⇨ _____

↺_____↻

↺_____↻

John says to Mary, "I like your hair." Mary smiles and says, "Thank you."

a. message
b. sender
c. receiver
d. feedback - verbal
e. feedback - nonverbal

E

Parent Conference

Objective:

To improve home/school relationships by making the point conference more effective.

Time:

Part of one session

Materials:

One "Conference Information Sheet" for each advisee

Procedures:

This is an excellent activity for the session before Open House or regular parent conferences. Parent conferences can be stressful experiences for students, parents, and advisors — but they need not be. Conferences can be very positive and pleasant and the use of the Conference Information Sheet will help to achieve this goal.

This activity provides both students and parents an opportunity to think over what items *they* would like to include on the parent conference agenda. This preparation has the added benefits of:
(a) letting the advisor know *in advance* what concerns he will be asked to deal with, and
(b) providing her time to do the research and materials gathering necessary to conduct the conference smoothly.

Distrubute the sheets to each advisee, explaining that you would like them to fill out the top half now and then to take the sheet home for their parents to complete. Ask that they return the sheets within two days.

Conference Information Sheet

Adviser's Name _____

Parent conferences are most successful when parents, students, and advisers all have the opportunity to plan in advance some of the items to be discussed. Students should fill out the first section of the form and have their parents fill out the second section. Please return the form to your adviser within two days. (Parents may mail the form directly to the adviser if they prefer.)

Advisee Section

1. One good thing that happened to me recently that I hope my adviser will tell my parents about is _____

2. I think my adviser knows how much I've progressed in _____

3. _____ is the area I've worked the hardest in this semester.

4. A class in which the teacher really understands me is _____

5. I hope my parents and my adviser get a chance to talk about _____

6. I wish my parents would explain to my adviser about _____

7. I wish my adviser would explain to my parents about _____

8. I'd like my parents' help with _____

9. One thing that worries me about parents talking to my adviser is _____

_____ Other: _____

Parent Section

1. One thing I don't understand about this school's program is _____

2. I do have this concern about homework: _____
_____

3. One thing I wonder about my son's/daughter's behavior in school is _____

4. In the area of basic skills (reading, language, and math), I wonder... _____

5. One aspect of my son's/daughter's character that I wish the school understood better is _____

6. I'd like to hear about the strengths the school sees in my student in the area(s) of _____

7. I wish I had better information about _____

8. I could help my student more if _____

9. Please list other topics you wish to discuss on a separate sheet.

Action — Reaction – Consequence

Objectives:
To help students recognize that actions always result in some other actions.

Time:
One session

Materials:
Worksheet: "What Might Happen?"

Procedures:

1. Make a general introduction regarding actions and results of other actions or reactions. Give a couple of examples.

2. Pass out worksheet of situations which can be done verbally with the whole group, orally in pairs or small groups, or as a written assignment.

3. In closing discussion reemphasize the idea of accepting responsibility for one's own behavior.

???

WHAT MIGHT HAPPEN...?

1. Your parents decide to adopt a new brother or sister. What are some things that might happen?

2. You brought a lost animal home with you. What are some things that might happen?

3. You are seen taking something that belongs to someone else. What are some things that might happen?

4. You yelled at your mother. What are some things that might happen?

5. Your friend asks you to help him with his work all the time. What are some things that might happen?

6. You didn't finish your homework. What are some things that might happen?

7. You choose Home Economics and French for two of your electives next year. What are some things that might happen?

8. You leave school without telling anyone and someone sees you. What are some things that might happen?

9. You bump into a teacher carrying a huge stack of paper. What are some things that might happen?

10. Your brakes failed while driving down the hill. What are some things that might happen?

11. You wake up one morning and find that you have turned into a rabbit. What are some things that might happen?

12. You are sent to the store and while paying for your groceries, you discover you do not have enough money. What are some things that might happen?

13. You choose chorus and American politics for your electives next year. What are some things that might happen?

14. Your best friend is mad at you. You write your friend a note saying you are sorry and want to make up. What are some things that might happen?

15. There is a shortage of teachers. Your school, with the same number of students, will have only half as many teachers next year. What are some things that might happen?

16. The wage earner (or earners) in your family has lost his/her job. What happens now?

???

F

Male/Female

Objective:
To help students understand the concept of stereotyping and its effects on people.

Time:
One session

Materials:
Journals or paper/pencil

Procedures:

Discuss how we tend to stereotype people — especially into male/female jobs, characteristics, hobbies, etc. Advisor might share some former restrictions and/or stereotypes that have been eliminated since WWII.

Place the following open-ended sentences on the board. Ask students to respond to several of the items by writing in their journals or on a separate sheet of paper:

1. As a child I was happy that I was a girl/boy because:

2. As a child I wished I were a boy/girl (opposite sex) because:

3. The experiences I enjoyed most as a child were:

   How would I have experienced these if I had been a girl/boy (opposite sex)

4. As an adult man/woman I feel:

5. As an adult man/woman I would like my daughter to know: My son to know:

Wrap-up:

For follow-up, students might enjoy sharing their responses and list ideas that they included in their journals.

Stereotypes and Human Differences

Objective:
To help students recognize that differences in cultural and ethnic backgrounds can cause misunderstandings.

Time:
Two sessions

Materials:
"Stereotypes of People," Individual Choice Sheet"
and "Group Choice Sheet"

Procedures:

SESSION 1

1. Pass out the Stereotypes of People sheet and ask students to read along as the teacher reads this situation. Check for questions and language problems.

2. Pass out Individual Choice Sheets and ask students to complete them.

3. Take time to discuss the choices.

SESSION 2

Organize groups and complete Group Choice Sheet

CLOSURE:

1. What kinds of cultural differences have you experienced?

2. What fears come from people new or unfamiliar to us?

3. What is a stereotype example?

Stereotypes of People

Lincoln Middle School is located in a large eastern city. When Lincoln first opened about five years ago, all of the students enrolled were North Americans.

Not that there weren't any differences among the students who attended Lincoln. Some of Lincoln's students came from wealthy families, others came from families that had very little money. Most came from families that were in-between — neither wealthy nor poor.

For the last two years, a new group of students has been attending Lincoln. Each year there are more of these students — children of parents who were raised in Latin America.

Recently, teachers have begun to complain about this new group of students.

These Latin American students all want to sit together. They don't want to make friends with North American students.

These Latin American students refuse to work on group projects with North American students. It is almost impossible to get them to cooperate. They are always bickering.

My Latin American students have got chips on their shoulders. They are ready to fight with other students at the drop of a hat.

Mr. Ross, the principal, decided to share his problem with a woman at the local university, an anthropologist. The professor with whom he talked studies different aspects of Latin American life.

When Mr. Ross explained his problem, the professor said, "Part of your problem is that North American teachers believe a lot of bad things about Latin Americans. If you can remove these stereotypes, it will help you solve your problem. There will be less conflict between North American and Latin American students."

Mr. Ross then asked the professor, "What stereotypes about North Americans are held by Latin Americans?"

Individual Choice Sheet

The professor identified nine stereotypes of North Americans that Latin Americans tend to believe. Rank order these from the stereotype that would be most harmful to Latin Americans and North Americans who would like to be friends. Place a "1" by the most harmful stereotype, a "2" by the next most harmful one. Continue to rank the stereotypes until you have placed a "9" by the least harmful stereotype.

_____ In North America, nearly all the people are violent. The gangster is a hero in North America.

_____ In North America, nearly all the people want to get rich at the expense of Latin Americans.

_____ In North America, most young people are hippies who use drugs and do other bad things.

_____ In North America, most people are rich. They like to show off their wealth doing foolish things.

_____ In North America, most people are Protestants. They have no respect for the Catholic church.

_____ In North America, most people do not know how to use good manners. Wives do not keep houses neat. Table manners are poor.

_____ In North America, most people are racists. Blacks, Indians, and other minority groups have no chance to succeed.

_____ In North America, most people support dictators who rule in Latin America. They support democracy just for themselves.

_____ In North America, most people have no respect for traditional institutions — the home, the church, or the school.

Group Choice Sheet

Work with other members of your group to complete this choice sheet.

The three worst stereotypes are:

    A.

    B.

    C.

If these three stereotypes were removed, conditions at Lincoln would improve in the following ways.

We believe the three least harmful stereotypes are:

    A.

    B.

    C.

Now, imagine that the following conditions were true:
1. **All the stereotypes except the three you selected as least harmful have been removed at Lincoln.**

2. **The three you identified as least harmful are still believed by Latin Americans.**

If these conditions are true, how might these three stereotypes make it difficult for North American boys and girls to work with Latin American boys and girls?

Nevertheless, these three are least harmful because:

"Who?"

Objective:
To be able to predict the behavior of different types of people.

Time:
One session

Materials:
See below

Procedures:
A class set of "Character Sketches" (p.) is needed. Each of the responses (p.) should be on an index card — you will need as many cards as you have groups. Be sure to label cards as to responses to situation A, B, or C.

Break advisory group into small groups of four or five. Distribute Character Sketch sheets to each student. Have the three potential responses on separate cards. Say to the group: "I am going to describe a situation to you, and then I will give a card with a possible student response on it to someone in the room. He will read it out loud as realistically as possible. Then, it will be your group's job to try to agree on which student would be most likely to have responded in that way. When your group agrees, tell me *privately* which character your group votes for. Groups get five (5) points for each correct guess. At the end of the session, the group with the most points will be awarded honorary Ph.D.'s in Psychology."
(Note to advisor: Distribute and vote on only one card at a time.)

WRAP-UP:
Situation A:	Response X, Brian	
	Response Y, Randy	
	Response Z, Jake	
Situation B:	Response X, Charlie	
	Response Y, Angie	
	Response Z, Lloyd	
Situation C:	Response X, Anna	
	Response Y, Jody	
	Response Z, Jean	

NOTE: This answer key was developed in a subjective manner. Therefore credit should be given to a team if it provides sound reasoning for matching a response to a character other than listed in the key.

SITUATION A:

In the hall during passing time, Andy trips a person he hardly knows, causing that person to drop all of his books and bruise a knee. What is the response of the person who is tripped?

Character Sketch Sheet (Situation A)

1. *Brian* is manager of the track team. He is big, good-natured, and friendly with many kids. Brian feels good about himself and figures Andy likes him and was just goofing around.

2. *Randy* is always the victim of bullies. He is very quiet and often feels people take advantage of him.

3. *Jake* is smaller than other boys in his class. He feels like he has to prove that he is as tough as the rest of them. He is known for a short temper.

4. *Mark* is a good guy, but it really makes him mad when someone makes him look foolish. He'd like to punch Andy's face, but his parents told him that if he ever gets caught fighting in school, they will really lay into him.

5. *Jerry* is a new student from another state. He was very popular in his old school and would like to make a good impression here. However, he is not sure of how the students feel about him here.

SITUATION B:

A student in class receives an "F" grade on a test.

Character Sketch Sheet (Situation B)

1. *Larry* is a "C" student. He tries hard. He does not have many friends in class.

2. *Lloyd* is maintaining a "C" average in class. He relies on his friends in class to help him get answers on worksheets. He wants to keep his "C" but doesn't like to do much work on his own.

3. *Michele* is receiving "D" or "C" grades. She spends most of her time in class drawing pictures on her notebook, daydreaming, or talking to her friends. She doesn't like the teacher.

4. *Charlie* received four "Fs" on other tests this quarter. He does not like class or the teacher. Charlie was asked to leave the classroom on two previous occasions for smarting off to the teacher.

5. *Angie* is a very quiet "A" student. She usually works by herself and is very concerned about doing good work. She was sick the week before the test.

SITUATION C:

An eighth grade girl is smoking in the restroom between classes. Several other students are gathered around her talking. A teacher enters suddenly. In a panic to hide the cigarette, the girl passes it to the girl next to her. Unfortunately, the teacher sees the second girl with the cigarette and orders her to the main office for suspension from school for smoking. The girl says to the principal:

Character Sketch Sheet (Situation C)

1. *Paula* acts like she doesn't care about school or about teachers, but she really wants everyone to think well of her. She would never admit to her friends that she wishes she was an "A" student.

2. *Jean* hates school because everyone and everything there makes her feel dumb. She thinks teachers try to make her feel bad.

3. *Veronica* is an honor student and is well-liked by students and teachers. She is very considerate of other people's feelings and helps students who are slow learners. She feels good about school and her classmates.

4. *Ann* knows the kids call her "Big Anna" because they think she's tough, but she really would prefer to have them like her. Still, she does have a tendency to get loud when she's mad.

5. *Jody* is very quiet and shy. She tries hard in school and is always afraid of getting in trouble. When people get mad at her, she gets confused and cries.

SITUATION A	SITUATION A	SITUATION A
"Aw, cut it out man. You're going to make me late for class" He laughs, picks up his books and leaves for class.	"Leave me alone, you creep." He gathers his books and goes immediately to his next class, where he asks his teacher for a pass to the nurse.	"You aren't so tough. Come here, you big turkey, and I'll punch your lights out." He pushes Andy against a wall and a fight begins.
RESPONSE X	RESPONSE Y	RESPONSE Z
SITUATION B	SITUATION B	SITUATION B
"I hate this class — none of this junk matters to me!" (Said loud enough so everyone can hear.)	"Is there any make-up work or extra credit that I could do to make up this "F?" (Said to teacher.)	(Whines to teacher.) "This isn't fair. I didn't understand these questions. Can't I get some of my points back?"
RESPONSE X	RESPONSE Y	RESPONSE Z
SITUATION C	SITUATION C	SITUATION C
"I'm not going to take the rap for something I didn't do! Prove I was smoking — you can't, 'cause I wasn't. Just 'cause she saw the butt in my hand doesn't mean I was smoking. Anybody grabs something that somebody hands them. You can't help it. Now get off my back."	(Crying) "I'm really sorry I was holding the cigarette. Honest, I wasn't smoking. Someone just pushed it into my hand and then I was so scared, I didn't know what to do. Everyone just backed away from me. Please believe me."	"Hey, man, that wasn't me smokin'... You're probably gonna get down on me now just for getting caught holdin' someone else's cigarette. Schools are always like that. Why should anybody try?"
RESPONSE X	RESPONSE Y	RESPONSE Z

Bank Robbery — A Group Solution

(a real challenge for a group)

Objective:
To emphasize the importance of contributions and insights from each member in a group and to experience the necessity for group organization in order to accomplish a task.

Time:
One- or two sessions

Materials:
Clues, each on a separate piece of paper.

Procedures:

1. Seat participants in a circle.
2. Give the following explanation to the group:
    Each of the pieces of paper I am holding contains one clue which will help you solve a bank robbery. If you put all the clues together, you will be able to solve the robbery. Any time you think you know the answer and the group agrees on the guess, you may tell me. I will only tell you whether your answer is right or wrong. If part of your answer is incorrect, I will not tell you which part it is.

    All sharing of clues and ideas must be done verbally. You may not pass your clues around or show them to anyone else, and you may not leave your seats to walk around the group.
3. After clarifying the rules, the instructor distributes the clues around the circle. If there are extra clues, continue dealing them around the circle until all clues are distributed.
4. The instructor states the task:
    The First National Bank of Minnetonka, Minnesota was robbed of one million dollars. You are to discover what person or persons did it.

    Once the group has started, the instructor should not assist students in any way. However, if groups are experiencing difficulty in finding a solution, you may want to let them write the clues out.
5. The solution to the robbery is:
    The Ellingtons collaborated to rob the bank. Miss Ellington supplies the front door key (borrowed from Mr. Greenbags) and Howard supplied the dynamite. Greenbags had already left for Brazil when the robbery took place. Mr. Smith was in Dogwalk the night of the robbery. Dirsey Flowers was at the home of Anastasia's parents. The Ellingtons were lying when they tried to implicate Smith.

6. Following the accurate solution to the robbery, the group should discuss:
    a. What behaviors contributed positively toward accomplishing the task?
    b. What behaviors hindered the accomplishment of the task?
    c. What are some of the things a group can do to facilitate the accomplishment of a task?

BANK ROBBERY CLUES
(cut into separate strips)

The robbery was discovered at 8:00 a.m. on Friday, November 12. The bank had closed at 5:00 p.m. the previous day.

Miss Margaret Ellington, a teller at the bank, discovered the robbery.

The vault of the bank had been blasted open by dynamite.

The president of the bank, Mr. Albert Greenbags, left before the robbery was discovered. He was arrested by authorities at the Mexico City airport at noon on Friday, November 12.

The president of the bank had been having trouble with his wife, who spent all of his money. He had frequently talked of leaving her.

The front door of the bank had been opened with a key.

The only keys to the bank were held by the janitor and the president of the bank.

Miss Ellington often borrowed the president's key to open the bank early when she had an extra amount of work to do.

A strange, hippie-type person had been hanging around the bank on Thursday, November 11, watching employees and customers.

A substantial amount of dynamite had been stolen from the Acme Construction Company on Wednesday, November 10.

An Acme employee, Howard Ellington, said that a hippie had been hanging around the construction company on Wednesday afternoon.

The hippie-type character, whose name was Dirsey Flowers and who had recently dropped out of Southwest Arkansas State College, was found by police in East Birdwatch, about ten miles from Minnetonka.

Dirsey Flowers was carrying $500 when police apprehended him and had thrown a package into the river as the police approached.

Anastasia Wallflower of East Birdwatch, Wisconsin, said that she had bought $500 worth of genuine Indian love beads from Dirsey Flowers for resale in her boutique in downtown East Birdwatch.

Anastasia said that Dirsey had spent the night of November 11th at the home of her parents and left after a pleasant breakfast on the morning of the 12th.

When police tried to locate the janitor of the bank, Elwood Smith, he had apparently disappeared.

Miss Ellington stated that her brother, Howard, when strolling to Taylor's Diner for coffee about 11:00 p.m. on Thursday, November 11, had seen Mr. Smith running from the bank.

Mr. Smith was found by the F.B.I. in Dogwalk, Georgia, on November 12. He had arrived there via Southern Airlines Flight 414 at 5:00 pm. on the 11th.

The airline clerk confirmed the time of Smith's arrival.

Mr. Greenbags was the only person who had a key to the vault.

There were no planes out of Dogwalk between 4:00 pm. and 7:00 a.m.

In addition to keeping payroll records, Mr. Willington was in charge of the dynamite supplies of the Acme Construction Company.

Miss Ellington said that Mr. Smith had often flirted with her.

Mr. Smith's father, a gold prospector in Alaska, had died in September.

Mr. Greenbags waited in the terminal at O'Hare Field in Chicago for 16 hours because of engine trouble on the plane he was to take to Mexico City.

Farmer Brown/Farmer Jones

Objectives:

To listen astutely. To be open-minded. To arrive at consensus through small group interaction before settling on one answer for the entire group.

Time:

One or two sessions

Procedures:

Group members are presented with a problem which must be collectively solved by arriving at a consensus within the large group. Read the problem once. Repeat it only once after the directions if necessary. Do not answer any questions or allow the group members to use pen or pencil throughout this entire exercise. After reading the problem give the following directions:

1. This problem has only one correct answer.
2. You must solve the problem orally — no pencils or paper.
3. Think. Ask for ideas and answers. Be open-minded.
4. As the group attempts to solve this problem, all people who think that Farmer Brown is ahead by $30, form a group; all who think that Jones is ahead by $10, form a group; and so on. Form as many small groups as you have answers. Undecided people should form their own group. Any time that you feel that your group is wrong, join the group that you feel has the correct answer. Each group that is positive that it has the correct answer should try to convince the other groups to agree with it until all people agree on one answer.
5. When consensus is reached by each person within the entire group, a group spokesperson should indicate what the answer is. I will answer "yes" or "no." If the group has reached the wrong answer, start over.
6. Remember, consensus requires that each person agree with the final outcome. If you are dubious, don't allow others to coerce you to agree. Be convinced that the answer is one that you agree with.
After the correct answer has been arrived at, discuss the process.

(This activity is a good follow-up for the murder mystery activity or other listening activities that emphasize many of the same skills.)

Problem: Farmer Brown/Farmer Jones

Farmer Jones was walking along a road past Farmer Brown's field. He saw a pony that he took a fancy to, went in, and paid Farmer Brown $60.00 for the pony. Farmer Brown later regretted selling his pony so he went to Farmer Jones and bought back the pony for $70.00. Farmer Jones thought it over, deciding that he really wanted that pony so he went back to Farmer Brown and paid $80.00 for the pony. Finally, Farmer Brown decided that he had had enough. He decided that he absolutely needed the pony and could never part with it again so he went and paid $90.00 for the pony.
Problem: Who came out ahead? By how much.

G

Solve the Mystery

Objectives:
Students will learn to listen carefully, select pertinent information, learn to ask appropriate questions — and have fun!.

Time:
One session.

Materials:
Group leader needs copy of "Mysteries and Solutions"

Procedures:

1. Group leader presents one mystery at a timeto the group.

2. Students ask questions which can only be answered by *yes* or *no*. Using the answers, try to solve the mystery.

Variations:

1. Each student can ask only one question until all have had a chance (have someone write names on board.)

2. Appoint one person to be class recorder and put information used on the board.

Mysteries and Solutions

Mysteries

1. A dead man was found lying face down in the middle of a desert with a knapsack on his back. How did he die?

2. A man walked into a tavern and up to the bar. The bartender pulled out a gun and shot two bullets into the floor close to the man. The man said, "Thank you," and turned around and walked out. ("Thank you" were the only words used throughout this scene.) Why did the bartender shoot the gun, and why did the man say "thank you?"

3. Rob and Gina were found lying next to an open window. Near them was some broken glass and a puddle of water. How did they die?

4. Picture a small room with no windows and one door. At a table four hands of a card game had been dealt, but there are only three men at the table — all of them dead, but there is no evidence of violence. On a wall behind these men is a hook which is now empty. What happened here?

5. Mr. Smith was reading in the paper about a shipwreck in which there was only one fatality — Mrs. P.J. Jones. Although Mr. Smith had never even seen or met Mrs. P.J. Jones before, he knew that her death hadn't been accidental — she had been murdered. How did he know this?

6. A man living on the twelfth floor of an apartment building always rides the elevator down but takes the stairs up, unless it is raining. Why?

Solutions

1. The man jumped form an airplane and his parachute failed to open.

2. The man had the hiccups so the bartender cured them by shooting the gun. That's why the man thanked the bartender.

3. Rob and Gina were goldfish and they died from suffocation. A wind from the open window had blown their bowl over.

4. The room is in a submarine and the hook once held an oxygen tank, the only oxygen tank in the room. Four men had gambled for this tank because the air was running out in the room and the winner apparently left, leaving the other three behind to die of suffocation.

5. Mr. Smith was a travel agent and he remembered selling two tickets to Mr. P.J. Jones — one was a round trip and one was a one-way ticket.

6. He is a midget and is unable to reach button #12 on the elevator control panel unless he has his umbrella.

CLOSURE:
Why was forming good questions important in this activity?

G

The Baseball Team Exercise

Objective:
To work with others to find a solution to a problem.

Time:
One session

Materials:
A copy sheet of the information should be given to each group.

Procedures:

Divide the group into small groups of three. Each group is to determine from the given information who plays what position on a baseball team. See how long it takes each group to solve the problem The groups should review the ways they utilized information in solving the problem.

SOLUTION

Catcher: Allen

Pitcher: Harry

First Baseman: Leroy

Second Baseman: Jerry

Third Baseman: Andy

Shortstop: Ed

Left Field: Sam

Center Field: Sean

Right Field: Mike

WHO'S ON FIRST?

On the basis of the information provided below, determine who plays what position.

a. Andy dislikes the catcher.

b. Ed's sister is engaged to the second baseman.

c. The center fielder is taller than the right fielder.

d. Harry and the third baseman live in the same building.

e. Leroy and Allen each won $20 from the pitcher at pinochle.

f. Ed and the outfielders play poker during their free time.

g. The pitcher's wife is the third baseman's sister.

h. All the battery and the infield, except Allen, Harry and Andy, are shorter than Sam.

i. Leroy, Andy, and the shortstop lost $150 each at the racetrack.

j. Leroy, Harry, Sean, and the catcher took a trouncing from the second baseman at pool.

k. Sam is undergoing a divorce suit.

l. The catcher and the third baseman each have two children.

m. Ed, Leroy, Jerry, and the right fielder and center fielder are bachelors; the others are married.

n. The shortstop, the third baseman, and Sean each won $100 betting on the fights.

o. One of the outfielders is either Mike or Andy.

p. Jerry is taller than Sean; Mike is shorter than Bill. Each of them is heavier than the third baseman.

G

Inventing and Selling Activity

Objective:
To explore the creativity of a group in a problem-solving situation.

Time:

Two or three sessions

Materials:

A paper sack of "junk" materials for each small group. (Have kids bring the "junk" several days in advance.) Each sack can contain one item or several items.

Procedures:

1. Put paper sacks in center of large group.

2. Divide in small groups of 3 or 4. Each group takes one paper sack.

3. The group task is to invent something for use in the school or home, using the item or items in the sack. The group is free to use other small materials that can be scavenged from the immediate area, but the item in the sack should be the major element of the invention.

4. The second part of the task is for each small group to prepare an advertisement or "sales pitch" for the item.

5. The total group gathers together in a circle so each small group can display its product and present its sales pitch.

Experiment in Problem Solving

Objectives:

To study the sharing of information in task-oriented groups and focus on cooperation

Time: **Materials:**

Two sessions   Class set of problem solving task instructions.
                                     Information for individual group members
                                     Set of 26, 3" X 5" cards for each group.

Procedures:

1. Have each small group choose a leader. Give the leader the problem solving task instruction sheets for distribution to the group members. The leader should also be given the information cards.

2. After group members have had sufficient time to read the instruction sheet, the leader distributes the information cards randomly among the members of the group. When cards are distributed, announce that time begins. Note time on the board.

3. After 20 minutes (or less if the groups finish early) call time.

4. The smaller groups then discuss their reactions to the problem solving activity. Stress in this discussion should be placed on the *processing of information* and the *sharing of leadership in task situations*.

5. After approximately 5 minutes of discussion, the smaller groups form one large circle and share insights gained in the smaller groups with the whole group.

6. The solution to the problem is 20/30 "wors."

Instructions

Pretend that *lutts* and *mipps* represent a new way of measuring distance, and that *dars, wors,* and *mirs* represent a new way of measuring time. A man drives from Town A through Town B and Town C to Town D. The task of your group is to determine how many *wors* the entire trip took. You have 20 minutes for this task. Do not choose a formal leader.

You will be given cards containing information related to the task of the group. You may share this information orally, but you must keep the cards in your hands throughout.

Information for Group Members

Cut these bits of information or questions into strips for random distribution to task groups:

How far is it from A to B?

It is 4 lutts from A to B.

How far is it from B to C?

It is 8 lutts from B to C.

How far is it from C to D?

It is 10 lutts from C to D.

What is a lutt?

A lutt is 10 mipps.

What is a mipp?

A mipp is a way of measuring distance.

How many mipps are there in a mile?

There are 2 mipps in a mile.

What is a dar?

A dar is 10 wors.

What is a wor?

A wor is 5 mirs.

What is a mir?

A mir is a way of measuring time.

How many mirs are there in an hour?

There are 2 mirs in an hour.

How fast does the man drive from A to B?

The man drives from A to B at the rate of 24 lutts per wor.

How fast does the man drive from B to C?

The man drives from B to C at the rate of 30 lutts per wor.

How fast does the man drive from C to D?

The man drives from C to D at the rate of 30 lutts per wor.

H

Sharing Through Food Baskets

Objective:
To provide an opportunity for students to share with those in need.

Time:
Parts of various sessions

Materials:
Large box with paper, tape, colored markers, stickers, and pictures to decorate, etc.

Procedures:

Discuss with students the possibility fo providing support to a family in need by donating items for a food basket. If interest is sufficient encourage them to bring in non-perishable items on a selected day or any day during a designated week. Any individual or small group may volunteer to decorate the box, making it as attractive as possible. Another student could write a note to be included with the food basket. It is important that every child be involved in this activity so that all will feel a sense of ownership and pride in the outcome.

After food has been collected and arranged attractively in the box, it should be delivered to a local food shelf, church organization, or designated family in the community who is in need. Confidentiality of the receiver must be respected, of course. A proper recipient or agency should be contacted before the activity is initiated.

NOTE: The advisory groups may choose to repeat this activity at Christmas, Easter, or Thanksgiving in keeping with the holiday spirit of sharing and caring.

Discuss with students how they felt about participating in this project, using such questions as the following::

1. Which is more satisfying — to give or to receive?
2. Can you think of a time when it was better to give? When was it better to receive?
3. Why is it hard for some people to accept charity from others?

H

Adopt a Grandparent

Objective:
To help students become more sensitive to the problems and needs of the elderly.

Time:
Ongoing at least for one quarter.

Materials:
Paper, pens, envelopes

Procedures:

The teacher should contact a local nursing home and make arrangements with the Activity Director to implement an exchange of letters between advisory students and selected residents. Request a very brief biography of each senior citizen so that students might have a basis on which to choose their adopted grandparent. Make certain that there is a "grandparent" for every student.

Introduce the activity to the advisory group by discussing some of the problems facing elderly people in our society today. Responses might include the following: poverty, loneliness, social isolation, loss of status or respect, feelings of worthlessness, poor health, etc. Some may have grandparents or great grandparents that are elderly and living in a nursing home.

Inform students that they are going to have an opportunity to make a difference in the lives of some elderly people when they 'adopt" a grandparent. They will get acquainted by writing letters on a regular basis to a selected person.

The advisor should briefly discuss the format of a friendly letter and provide students with a skeleton letter or outline to refer to during the quarter. Encourage them to send pictures of themselves whenever possible or add other personal touches to their letters.

The teacher will want to proof letters before mailing and students may edit each other's letters. A designated day should be set aside for this activity, and time also allowed later for sharing letters students may have received from the "grandparents."

Near the conclusion of this activity, if at all possible, the teacher should take students to meet with their "adopted grandparents" in the nursing home. At the end of this activity, the teacher should discuss the following questions with the group:

How did you feel about "adopting" someone in the nursing home?

Did your opinion change of elderly people after participating through letters or meeting with your "grandparent?" In what way?

What did you learn about yourself from this activity? What did you learn about others?

(continued)

What was the highlight for you of being involved in this activity?

What suggestions could you make to help older people feel less lonely and isolated in their communities?

NOTE: Encourage students to continue their letter-writing after this activity is culminated. Some students may choose to get their families involved and may visit the nursing home as a family unit. The bonding that takes place between the student and the senior citizen may last a long time, fulfilling a need in both of their lives.

SAMPLE LETTER OUTLINE

> 123 Fourth Street
> Anoka, Minnesota
> October 1, 1991
>
> **Dear Adopted Grandparent, (Mrs. Brown, Mr. Smith, etc.)**
>
> **Introduce yourself, sharing things about your family, hobbies, school experiences, pets, etc.**
>
> **Ask questions to show your interest, based on information given in the biographical sketch sent from the nursing home. Do not ask personal things that could be embarrassing to your grandparent.**
>
> **Make your letters pleasant and cheerful. Write clearly in ink so that they can be easily read. (A first draft can be in pencil so it can more easily be altered.)**
>
> **Be sure you have good margins on both sides of the paper. Write on one side of the paper only.**
>
> **Let your grandparent know that you would enjoy his/her letters and look forward to receiving them.**
>
> > **Your friend,**
> > **Cheryl Clark**

SAMPLE ADDRESSED ENVELOPE

Your name and address should be written in the upper left hand corner of the envelope.

> **Greg Smith**
> **1234 Fifth Street**
> **Washington, DC 21005**
>
> > **Mrs. John Anderson**
> > **Grandview Nursing Home**
> > **Washington, DC 21005**

H

Storybooks for Tots

Objective:
To offer students the opportunity to experience the joy of sharing by preparing storybooks to be donated to a children's hospital or other agency.

Time:
Four to six sessions

Materials:
Paper, pencil, pen, markers, colors, glue, scissors, magazines, construction paper, stencils, yarn, other special items according to preference of each pair of students.

Procedures:

Offer students the opportunity to become authors of children's books, which will be donated to a hospital, day care center, or elementary classroom in the school district.

Discuss the elements that would appeal to a young child who might read the book:
1. Simple story
2. Short sentences
3. Colorful pictures or illustrations
4. Words easy to understand.
5. Attractive, eye-catching cover, etc.

Ask students to pair up for this activity, although anyone who wishes to work alone should be given this opportunity. In the pair groups, students should discuss ideas for the plot of their storybook. When a subject is agreed upon, students can decide if one person is going to do the writing and the other draw the illustrations, or perhaps the work will be divided so that each student will do half the writing and illustrating. Give the students flexibility to decide how the work will be distributed.

Students should write no more than two or three sentences of the story on a single page. Standard 8 1/2 X 11 paper folded in half will make a nice little book. A cover should be made out of construction paper or other stock, with the authors' names and title of the book. Students may also want to include a dedication page to someone special.

The first drafts should be written in pencil so that corrections and improvements can be made before the final copy is written in ink. Either the teacher or another adult should edit the story before it is ready for the final printing.

Once the story lines have been finished, illustrations can be created and placed on appropriate pages. Encourage students to use as many of these as possible, preferably one on each page. Pictures cut out of magazines can be used although original art work is preferable.

A follow-up discussion after the books have been donated would be appropriate using such questions as:
1. What did you enjoy most about this project?
2. How did you feel when you book was finished?
3. What did you learn about yourself and others from this activity?

Bonus Mind Teasers

Can you change a dollar into 50 coins?

Can you arrange eight 8's to total 1,000?

Can you divide a square into six perfect squares?

Can you make 5 odd numbers add up to 14?

Can you divide this plot into four pieces of equal size and shape with the same number of trees in each piece?

A Time Line of American History

Match the events in the right hand column with
the dates on left to create a modified time line.

1492___	a. Louisiana Purchase
1620___	b. Pearl Harbor
1776___	c. Viet Nam War ends
1803___	d. Civil War ends
1849___	e. WWI ends
1865___	f. Pilgrims land
1895___	g. President Kennedy assassinated
1918___	h. California Gold Rush
1929___	i. Watergate scandal — Nixon resigns
1941___	j. The Great Depression
1954___	k. Man lands on the moon
1969___	l. Declaration of Independence
1974___	m. Columbus discovers America
1975___	n. Supreme Court rules school segregation unconstitutional

Equation Analysis Test

This test does not measure your intelligence, your fluency with words, and certainly not your mathematical ability. It will, however, give you some gauge of your "mental flexibility" and creativity. Few people can solve more than half of the 24 questions on the first run-through. Many, however, reported getting answers long after the test had been set aside, and some reported solving all the items over a period of several days.

INSTRUCTIONS: Each item below contains the initials of words that will make it correct. Find the missing words. For example, 26 L of the A: would be 26 Letters of the Alphabet.

a. 26 L. of the A. _____

b. 7 W. of the W. _____

c. 1,001 A.N. _____

d. 12 S. of the Z. _____

e. 54 C. in a D. (with 2J.) _____

f. 9 P. in the S.S. _____

g. 88 P.K. _____

h. 13 S. on the A.F. _____

i. 32 D.F. at which W.F. _____
    _____

j. 18 H. on a G.C. _____

k. 90 D. in a R.A. _____

l. 200 D. for P.G. in M. _____
    _____

m. 8 S. on a S.S. _____

n. 3 B.M. (S,H,T.R.) _____

o. 4 Q. in a G. _____

p. 24 H. in a D. _____

q. 1 W. on a U. _____

r. 5 D. in a Z.C. _____

s. 57 H.V. _____

t. 11 P. on a F.T. _____

u. 1,000 W. that a P. is W. _____
    _____

v. 29 D. in F. in a L.Y. _____

w. 64 S. on a C.B. _____

x. 40 D. and N. of the G.F. _____
    _____